ORDINARY GRACE
WEEKS 18–34

ORDINARY GRACE
WEEKS 18–34

Daily Gospel Reflections

By the Daughters of St. Paul

Edited by Maria Grace Dateno, FSP
and Marianne Lorraine Trouvé, FSP

Pauline
BOOKS & MEDIA
Boston

Library of Congress Cataloging-in-Publication Data

Ordinary grace weeks 18–34 : daily Gospel reflections / by the Daughters of St. Paul ; edited by Maria Grace Dateno and Marianne Lorraine Trouvé.

　　p. cm.

ISBN 0-8198-5443-3 (pbk.)

1. Bible. N.T. Gospels--Devotional literature. 2. Catholic Church--Prayers and devotions. 3. Devotional calendars--Catholic Church. I. Dateno, Maria Grace. II. Trouvé, Marianne Lorraine. III. Daughters of St. Paul.

BS2555.54.O74 2011

242'.38--dc22

2010031638

Cover design by Rosana Usselmann

Cover photo by Mary Emmanuel Alves, FSP

Published by Pauline Books & Media, 50 Saint Pauls Avenue, Boston, MA 02130-3491

Printed in the U.S.A.

www.pauline.org

Pauline Books & Media is the publishing house of the Daughters of St. Paul, an international congregation of women religious serving the Church with the communications media.

1 2 3 4 5 6 7 8 9　　　　　　　　　15 14 13 12 11

Contents

᛫᛫᛫᛫᛫᛫᛫᛫᛫᛫᛫᛫

How to Use This Book

∴ · · · · · · · · · · · · ∴

*"Grace to you and peace from God our Father
and the Lord Jesus Christ" (Rom 1:7).*

Every day, God's grace is available through his word. There is, of course, nothing "ordinary" about grace, which is the amazing reality of God's life in us. There is nothing "ordinary" about Ordinary Time, either. In fact, the term "Ordinary Time" does not mean time that is average or mundane. It comes from the way the weeks are "ordered" using numbers in the form of ordinals (first, second, third, etc.).

Ordinary Time is a time of grace, an opportunity to reflect on all the aspects of the mystery of Christ, rather than intensely focusing on a certain aspect, as we do in the other liturgical seasons. You are invited to share with the Daughters of St. Paul their meditations on the Gospel readings of Ordinary Time.

These pages are based on *Lectio Divina* (holy reading), which is a way of praying with Scripture. Our founder, Blessed James Alberione, urged us to nourish ourselves with the Scriptures. He said that when we do this, we "experience interiorly the kindling of a divine fire." Many methods of *Lectio Divina* have developed since the time of early monasticism. Here, the sisters use a simple framework that allows the word of God to make room in our minds and hearts.

The first step, *Lectio* (reading), is to read the day's Gospel passage from a missal or Bible. Read it a few times slowly, perhaps especially noticing the phrase or verse that is listed under the *Meditatio* section.

Next, the *Meditatio* (meditation) expands the meaning of this phrase and explores what it is saying to us today—what God is asking of us, or challenging us to, or offering to us. After reading the meditation, take as much time as you wish to reflect on it.

The *Oratio* (prayer) can help you talk to God about what has arisen in your heart, so that the time of prayer becomes a conversation, not just a time to think. God has spoken in the Scripture. We hear the invitation in our meditation, but now a response is called for. Our response is not just to say, "Yes, I want to do as you are asking me," but also to say, "Help me do it, Lord!"

The short line under *Contemplatio* (contemplation) is a way of extending this time of prayer into life. You can silently repeat it throughout the day to help deepen the intimacy with the Lord that you experienced in prayer.

Thanks be to God!

Liturgical Calendar

⁘············⁘

Note to the reader: Each liturgical year the Church celebrates thirty-four weeks of Ordinary Time in two sections. This book picks up with the eighteenth week, which falls at the end of July/beginning of August. Ordinary Time continues until the first Sunday of Advent.

The following chart indicates the dates for the beginning of this book:

Year	Eighteenth Week Begins
2011	July 31
2012	August 5
2013	August 4
2014	August 3
2015	August 2
2016	July 31
2017	August 7 °
2018	August 5
2019	August 4
2020	August 2
2021	August 1
2022	July 31

* Sunday, August 6, is the Feast of the Transfiguration and takes the place of the Eighteenth Sunday of Ordinary Time this year. (See page 314.)

The Sunday readings follow a three-year cycle (A, B, or C) as indicated in the following chart:

Year	Cycle
2011	Cycle A
2012	Cycle B
2013	Cycle C
2014	Cycle A
2015	Cycle B
2016	Cycle C
2017	Cycle A
2018	Cycle B
2019	Cycle C
2020	Cycle A
2021	Cycle B
2022	Cycle C

Eighteenth Sunday of Ordinary Time— Year A

❖ · · · · · · · · · · · · ❖

Lectio

Matthew 14:13–21

Meditatio

> *"Give them some food yourselves."*

In today's Gospel, the disciples approach Jesus to remind him that the people need to eat. The disciples are probably so concerned about the crowd's hunger because they are hungry too. They have all endured a long day in this "deserted place." Because the disciples choose to give Jesus their own meager food, they must have had a fundamental trust in Jesus to provide for their needs. They could have tried to hide the food for themselves, but the Gospel simply reports that the disciples give Jesus their "five loaves and two fish." After Jesus blesses the food and gives it back to his disciples, they freely give it away to the crowds.

Like the disciples in today's Gospel, I can only share in Jesus' ministry of feeding and caring for his people when I generously give the Lord all that I have, even if it seems as insignificant as five loaves and two fish. The Lord takes me as I am, multiplies my gifts, and gives it all back to me a hundredfold. But this passage also reminds me that I am not meant to keep the Lord's gifts for myself. I receive the Lord's abundance so that I might freely share it with his people. I pray that I may grow in responding generously to the Lord as he shows me how he wants to bring life and love to others through me. Sometimes this may mean bringing food and physical life, but often it means offering a good word, a listening ear, or a supportive presence. When I live these simple daily actions with the Lord, they can become the ways in which God feeds and loves his people through me.

Oratio

Jesus, you know how often I try to reason through situations, trusting in myself and in my own strength. Help me to move away from this way of thinking, acting, and praying, so that I can more completely depend on you. May I bring to you my problems and concerns for myself and those I love. I believe you give me the strength to live each day as your disciple, in the midst of the difficulties I face along the way. Help me to be generous in sharing with others the good things you have given me, and to believe that you will always provide me with all that I need.

Contemplatio

"Do whatever he tells you" (Jn 2:5).

Eighteenth Sunday of Ordinary Time— Year B

∶············∶

Lectio

John 6:24–35

Meditatio

> *". . . they . . . came to Capernaum looking for Jesus."*

Today, we read about the crowd's response when they discover that Jesus and his disciples have crossed to the other side of the sea. They follow them and ask, "Rabbi, when did you get here?" They had just experienced one of Jesus' most amazing miracles, the feeding of the five thousand. Yet it isn't enough. They want more. So, they cross the sea to find him.

I've always wondered if they really knew what they were searching for. Jesus chides them for seeking the wrong things. They had just received a free meal. Their stomachs are full and their souls are touched, but do they know that they need Jesus' words, compassion, and presence? They need the Master to help them understand their deeper desires.

We often go about our daily lives doing what we need to do, what's expected of us, what we think will give us fulfillment. Yet in our very depths we feel an ache, a desire that keeps gnawing at us. Do we understand what we are feeling underneath all the externals? Have we ever really quieted ourselves enough to reflect and examine what that desire is? We long for intimacy, but can another person really fulfill our deepest desires? We long for communion, but can we ever find complete harmony and unity with others? By giving us his very self, his body and blood, Jesus answers this most basic need of the human soul—the need for love. "No one has greater love than this, to lay down one's life for one's friends" (Jn 15:13). Our souls yearn for love. The Eucharistic sacrifice of Christ is the perfect expression of love. By giving us himself as the Bread of Life, he is offering to us this most enduring and fulfilling of all loves. Let us look into our hearts and ask the Master for the grace to recognize our need for him to fulfill our genuine desires for love.

Oratio

Master of Love and Bread of Life, come and fill my soul with your presence. I want so many things, and I often put a lot of effort into fulfilling my desires, looking for new places and experiences. But what do I really want, deep down? Help me know and believe that only you can answer the desires and longings of my heart. I surrender my life to your love.

Contemplatio

"Those who seek the LORD lack no good thing" (Ps 34:11).

Eighteenth Sunday of Ordinary Time—
Year C

:·············:

Lectio

Luke 12:13–21

Meditatio

> *". . . life does not consist of possessions."*

The story in Luke sounds all too familiar—relatives fighting over an inheritance. Sometimes it seems as if claimants think the money is owed to them. "I want what is coming to me." Jesus calls it what it is: greed. Possessions are what we have, not who we are. In fact, even the poor can be greedy. Jesus reminds us that "life does not consist of possessions." To illustrate his point he tells a story. A rich farmer (note the man is already rich) has a wonderful year with an abundant harvest. His only problem is where to store it. His solution: build a larger facility. "I'll tear down the old buildings and put up bigger, better ones, and then I'll take it easy."

Greed, injustice to workers, neglect of land, wasting one's own productive years in laziness or by the idleness of an early and unproductive retirement—all of these are reflected in what the rich man plans to do, without realizing that his last moment is coming. "Your life will be required of you this very night." The end is coming suddenly, so he can't fudge intentions. He is caught in his greed and laziness. When there is no concern for others, the judgment will always come as a surprise. It is always so for those "who store up treasure for themselves but are not rich in what matters to God." Jesus already said that God isn't concerned with what we possess, and that we can't take any of it with us to the Great Accounting. All we can take is who we are. That is what matters to God. What riches, then, is he looking for? God values one who is rich in love of God and concern for others. These unseen treasures are our only inheritance. This is what Jesus meant when he said that the poor in spirit are blessed (see Mt 5:3).

Oratio

Jesus, Lord of all, you chose to give us a living example of the beauty and value of poverty, that true poverty of the spirit. Not only were you divested of the very glory and grandeur of your heavenly home, but you were born a poor, homeless child placed by your loving parents in an animals' feeding trough. You were chased and harassed throughout your early years. For announcing the Good News, healing, and praying, your own people rewarded you with the death of a dispossessed criminal. Accept my humble gift of a heart bent on imitating your total self-gift, a spirit poor but blessed. Amen.

Contemplatio

"Take care to guard against all greed."

Monday of the Eighteenth Week
of Ordinary Time

∴ · · · · · · · · · · · · ∴

Lectio

Matthew 14:13–21

Meditatio

> "*. . . give them some food yourselves.*"

By placing this rural event right after his flashback to the martyrdom of John the Baptist, Matthew achieves a stark contrast. Two banquets are portrayed—one in a fortress, attended only by the elite and featuring sensuality and death; the other in the open air, attended by anyone/everyone and featuring healing and life. The multiplication of the loaves is more or less the midpoint in a long trajectory that began with the manna in the desert and continued with the multiplication of barley loaves by the prophet Elisha. The scene in the hills of Galilee looks forward to the Last Supper and the Church's Eucharist, as well as the heavenly banquet mentioned in Isaiah 25:6 and Matthew 8:11–12.

Rereading this passage, I was drawn to Jesus' command to his disciples: "There is no need for them to go away; give them some food yourselves." The disciples show Jesus the little food they have. Acting in the role of the father of a Jewish family, Jesus takes the bread, says the blessing, breaks the bread, and hands it back to his disciples to distribute.

Mysteriously, there is enough bread for everyone, just as in the future the divine-human *presence of Jesus* would be mysteriously multiplied in the Eucharist, so that all the faithful can be nourished with the bread of life.

Thinking of the disciples' role in this, I remembered reading or hearing more than once that our poor prayers, our half-hearted sacrifices, our small acts of kindness can be multiplied by the Lord, as if zeroes were being added to the number 1. We give our "little," and the Lord makes that small contribution bear much fruit for his people. Jesus asks our cooperation, then he does the rest, just as he did with the disciples.

Oratio

Lord Jesus, help me to remember the importance of my small contributions, whatever they may be. When overcome by "weariness in well-doing," I want to keep in mind the disciples, who, until everyone had been fed, kept distributing the bread you had blessed and broken for the crowd. Help me to realize that the little I do has a much fuller meaning than I could ever imagine—a meaning I may never understand in this life, but will make me very happy in the next. Don't let me get discouraged, thinking I'm not getting anywhere. Help me to move ahead with purer motives and a lighter heart. Amen.

Contemplatio

"There is no need for them to go away."

Tuesday of the Eighteenth Week
of Ordinary Time

⁝·············⁝

Lectio

Matthew 14:22–36

Meditatio

> *"Immediately Jesus stretched out his hand and caught him. . . ."*

This moment in the life of Jesus calls to mind a painting by Sieger Köder called *Stronghold*. In the background, the disciples are in their little fishing boat, with the vast, tempestuous sea surrounding them. Very prominently in the foreground, Peter's hands are visible, firmly clasping the hand of Jesus. In my life of faith, these clasped hands provide a firm and important reminder that God is our sure refuge, and that he is always in control. If I call to him in need, he has only to reach out his hand.

It is a telling moment. We know from the Gospel that it is only when Peter takes his eyes off Jesus and sees "how strong the wind was" that he begins to sink. Perhaps you, too, can relate to Peter and have experienced dark moments when sinking felt inevitable. Yet, when I look over the darker moments in my own life, it becomes clear that when I fix my gaze on Christ, I have a very different perspective than when I focus on the people, events, or circumstances around me.

Fear and panic only set in if I lose my focus on that fixed point of reference—the face of Christ. If I gaze at him, I can maintain a sense of serenity and peace, even in the midst of the storm. Peace is a gift of the Holy Spirit—and no person or event can take it away from us. Growing in this awareness leaves us with a choice and a growing freedom. Nonetheless, when it is dark, it is perhaps even more important to remember another lesson from the Gospel: "*Immediately* Jesus stretched out his hand and caught him." Even though Peter takes his eyes off Jesus, Jesus never takes his eyes off Peter. He is with him, and for him, the whole time. Appearances can be deceiving. Like Peter, we, too, are always held safe in the hands of a loving God.

Oratio

Lord, when I am going through the turbulence of emotionally intense times, help me to remember your lesson for Peter on the stormy seas. You are always with me—and if I can only keep my eyes on you, it is possible for me to walk on water. The wind and the waves are the illusion of a life out of control, while your presence is the reality that grounds me, giving me courage and hope. In moments when the waves look too high and the wind feels too strong, help me to recall your faithful love and to place my trust firmly in you.

Contemplatio

I am safe in your hands.

Wednesday of the Eighteenth Week
Ordinary Time

∴ · · · · · · · · · · · ∴

Lectio

Matthew 15:21–28

Meditatio

"Have pity on me, Lord . . . help me."

Jesus and his disciples have entered a non-Jewish territory and a Canaanite woman is following him, crying out for help. But Jesus doesn't seem to notice. His disciples are annoyed because she keeps yelling after them and Jesus doesn't seem to care. They ask Jesus to send her away. Jesus tells the disciples that he has to focus on the "lost sheep of the house of Israel." This Canaanite woman exemplifies the virtue of fortitude. This mother pleads, begs, and insists that Jesus help her daughter. Jesus' response to her is shocking! "It is not right to take the food of the children and throw it to the dogs." My first reaction would be to run away sobbing, but this woman does not give up. She reminds me of Abraham bargaining with the Lord over the destruction of Sodom. Abraham walks along and tries to convince the Lord to spare the city for the sake of the innocent (see Gn 18:16–33).

The Canaanite woman refuses to back down until she receives a hearing. She acknowledges her need for Jesus. Although she tells Jesus about her daughter, she pleads mercy for herself. She is distraught by her daughter's illness and her own inability to help her. Her conversation with Jesus makes it seem as if he doesn't want to help her. I don't think Jesus would refuse anyone. Rather, I think that Jesus, knowing the desire of her heart, uses this situation to teach us a lesson. We may be tempted to feel helpless when facing a personal challenge or the illness of a loved one. We may feel we cannot ask for the Lord's help. May the example of the unnamed Canaanite woman give us the courage to hold on to hope. Let us call out to Jesus for his mercy and grace, knowing he will surely come to our aid.

Oratio

Lord, have mercy on me. Sometimes I feel so helpless in the situations that arise in my life. I am easily overwhelmed by the struggles and illnesses of my family and friends. May your living word give me the faith I need to believe in your love, to trust in your protection, and to hold on to hope.

Contemplatio

Lord, increase my faith.

Thursday of the Eighteenth Week of Ordinary Time

∴ · · · · · · · · · · · · ∴

Lectio

Matthew 16:13–23

Meditatio

> *" . . . who do you say that I am?"*

Jesus asks a penetrating question: "Who do you say that I am?" It may seem like an easy question, and we answer enthusiastically with Peter, "You are the Christ, the Son of the living God." But when we let Jesus' words permeate into the deepest core of our being, we realize that Jesus is asking about more than the words we say. He is asking about the message we speak with our lives. We declare with our lips that Jesus is Lord, but do we let him rule in every area of our lives? Do we obey, not only his commandments, but the inspirations to do good and avoid whatever would take us farther from him, even in small things? Or do we sometimes follow the voice of our modern culture more easily than that of Jesus?

It is so easy to let the world's voice drown out the Master's voice. Even Peter falters when Jesus speaks of his coming passion and death. "God forbid, Lord!" he exclaims. Peter had been open to the revelation of Christ's divinity, but he is closed to the revelation of his suffering. Jesus had also just said that he would rise on the third day, but Peter doesn't hear or understand that part. Because of his fear, Peter can't see ahead to Christ's promise of victory over death. It is so easy to be deceived by the voice of the world, urging us to follow the safer, more convenient path. It is so easy to take our eyes off Jesus and start to reason humanly. It is easy to follow Jesus in good times, but when suffering comes, we need to trust that Jesus will lead us through it to eternal joy in his kingdom. Despite Peter's faults, Jesus never took back his choice of Peter as head of his Church. This gives us reason to hope in the mercy of God.

Oratio

Lord, I believe that you are the Son of God. You are my life and my hope. I place my life entirely into your hands—past, present, and future. Let me see with your eyes and love with your heart. Let me follow your holy inspirations in all I do. Let my actions be consistent with the words I speak. Give me the grace to resist temptations and the allurements of this world and to never take my gaze from you.

Contemplatio

"My Lord and my God!" (Jn 20:28)

Friday of the Eighteenth Week
of Ordinary Time

⋮ · · · · · · · · · · · · ⋮

Lectio

Matthew 16:24–28

Meditatio

> *"Whoever wishes to come after me must . . .
> take up his cross, and follow me."*

Today, Jesus speaks to us, we who are his disciples. He explains that if we want to follow him, we must deny ourselves and take up our cross. Our cross includes the small and large sufferings we encounter each day. Suffering is not a uniquely Christian experience. Everyone suffers—those who are Jesus' disciples and those who are not. What might distinguish us, however, is *how* we suffer. We follow Jesus in the *way* we carry our cross and in our attitude toward suffering. Perhaps Jesus is inviting us to carry our cross with the same intentions he had when he carried his cross. Jesus suffered, died, and rose to redeem all people. Can we offer our sufferings, even the smallest, for this same intention? We might also have many other intentions: for peace, for our family, for an end to all violence and abortion, for the needs of the Church and the world—the list is endless.

Whatever suffering we encounter, we can turn to Jesus and unite it with his. This gives our suffering a redemptive value. In other words, joined with Jesus, our offering brings grace and salvation to others. When we reach heaven, a crowd of people might rush to greet and thank us for the graces we obtained for them in this way. Today's Gospel encourages us, for we are not alone as we carry our cross. We are following Jesus. Gradually we come to realize that he is walking with us as our companion and friend. He obtains for us the courage and strength we need. Jesus describes that glorious day when he will come in the glory of his Father, accompanied by his angels. Then he will reward us for following him. What a wonderful promise! On that day we will know the infinite value of following Jesus. We will bless the opportunities we had to carry our cross with Jesus.

Oratio

Jesus, you are my friend and teacher. You show me the value of embracing the crosses in my life. I want to take up my cross and accompany you. This is not easy. I do not like to suffer. Whether my crosses are small or large, enable me to unite them to your sufferings, and to believe that my sufferings have value. Remind me to renew the intentions for which I want to offer them. Give me the grace to continue to carry my cross, even when I feel pushed beyond what I can endure. Encourage me by reminding me of the reward that awaits me.

Contemplatio

Help me, Lord Jesus, to take up my cross today and to follow you.

Saturday of the Eighteenth Week of Ordinary Time

⁛ · · · · · · · · · · · · ⁛

Lectio

> Matthew 17:14–20

Meditatio

> *". . . if you have faith the size of a mustard seed. . . ."*

How small is a mustard seed? Many of us probably have no idea. We know, however, that it must be tiny from the way Jesus speaks of it here. In this reading, a distraught father kneels before Jesus, begging him to cure his son. The young man suffers from a mental illness, or worse yet, is possessed. He is so severely affected that he is in danger of losing control and drowning or burning himself. In desperation, the man adds that he brought his son to the disciples, but they could do nothing for him.

We are startled by what appears to be an angry reproach from Jesus. Is he exasperated with the disciples, the father, or the nearby crowd? He calls them "faithless" and "perverse." "How long will I be with you? How long will I endure you? Bring the boy here to me," he says. And with one reprimand, the demon comes out and the boy is cured. Embarrassed, the disciples quietly approach Jesus to ask why they could not expel the demon. We can imagine Jesus, still a little impatient, saying, "Because of your little faith." This reprimand may seem harsh. How many people can cure something this severe with just a word? Jesus thought that the disciples would understand better after having witnessed so many signs and wonders, and after having shared daily life with him for so long. If you have an iota of faith, "faith the size of a mustard seed . . . nothing will be impossible for you." Jesus points at the mountains and tells the disciples that with this living faith, they could actually move a mountain from one place to another by a mere word of command. Did Jesus mean this literally? Perhaps not, but he wants his disciples to realize that faith is a power; it is active prayer. Our faith, placed within his faith, will move the mountains in our lives. Nothing will be an obstacle to our union with God.

Oratio

Dear Jesus, today you have allowed us to be present in an intimate exchange between you and your disciples. You expose their weakness before us. As you correct and instruct them, we become aware that your words are directed at us, too. Faith is meant to be the watchword for Christians. If nothing else, we are to be people of faith, people who trust in the power of Christ in every event of life. Help us, Lord, to place all our trust in you. Amen.

Contemplatio

Jesus, all my trust is in you.

Nineteenth Sunday of Ordinary Time—
Year A

❧ · · · · · · · · · · · · ❧

Lectio

Matthew 14:22–33

Meditatio

"Take courage, it is I; do not be afraid."

As I pray with this Gospel account, I contemplate each part of it, entering into the story as if I too were with Peter and the other disciples in their boat. As they set off, the wind begins to rise, rocking their boat. In the heart of the night, as the wind tosses the disciples' boat, Jesus comes "toward them walking on the sea." I sense the fear that comes upon Peter and the disciples, but Jesus comforts and strengthens them, "Take courage, it is I; do not be afraid." Jesus does not scold Peter for his fear, but simply calls to him, "Come," thus inviting him to a deeper trust in Jesus and in his word. Peter leaves the security of his boat to follow Jesus. But when Peter takes his gaze off Jesus and looks around at the waves, seeing how strong the wind is, he starts to sink. But even in the midst of his panic and fear, Peter again turns his attention to Jesus, the only one who can save him. As soon as Peter cries out to Jesus, the Gospel tells us that "immediately" and without hesitation, "Jesus stretched out his hand and caught Peter."

This encounter allows Peter and the other disciples on the boat to more clearly recognize Jesus as the Son of God. But what about me? Just like Peter, how often I want proof: Is it really you, Jesus? Are you really with me? Jesus invites me also to deepen my faith in him, in whom we meet a God who loves us so much that he became one of us. He continues to come to me and to each of us today, in the midst of the darkest storms of life.

Oratio

Jesus, you know about all the storms in my life, all the uncertainties, trials, and suffering that I and those I love are going through. You know about all the fears and doubts I hold within, and how small and hopeless I am before them all. When I feel overwhelmed and afraid, and when I struggle to believe you are with me, help me to take courage from the knowledge that you are always with me. May I behold the greatness of your love that works with more power and beauty than I can imagine.

Contemplatio

"Be still and confess that I am God!" (Ps 46:11)

Ninteenth Sunday of Ordinary Time—
Year B

⟨⟩

Lectio

John 6:41–51

Meditatio

> *"No one can come to me unless the Father who sent me draw him."*

Jesus says these words during his discourse on the Bread of Life. One could state them positively as, "Everyone who comes to me comes because the Father is drawing him." In other words, our relationship with God—faith, the life of grace, prayer—is *all* a result of God's initiative, not ours. This was impressed upon me very clearly one year after a retreat. To begin my prayer times, I was using a short prayer as an invitation to Jesus to "come." I found it very helpful, but after using it for some months, it suddenly hit me that I had the wrong idea. I was not really the one inviting Jesus to come. Jesus was inviting *me*, and my prayer was the result of his initiative. I could pray "Come!" only because God had invited me first. *All* prayer—every time we turn to God—is a response to God's prior call and invitation.

So what difference does it make who starts it—whether we turn to God and initiate prayer or vice versa? Well, think of the difference between inviting someone to a party and being invited. It makes a lot of difference. If God is the one who invites me to prayer, then I'm not the hostess of the party; I don't have to make things happen. I just have to be present, attentive, and engaged, and what happens is up to God. Even though our part is a response to God's prior initiative, it is an indispensable part. Jesus says something along these lines when he later says to the apostles, "It was not you who chose me, but I who chose you" (Jn 15:16). He is the one who made the choice, but they did respond to his call.

Oratio

Jesus, thank you for this time of prayer. I am honored to be invited. Knowing that our relationship is based on your initiative takes the pressure off me. But you are an unusual host. Sometimes I come to pray and I am astonished by an insight or a strong experience of your love. Other times, it seems you've just planned a quiet moment for the two of us. And still other times it seems that you invited me, but then didn't show up yourself. That, however, is only what it *seems* like. I know and believe that you are right here with me, always.

Contemplatio

Draw me always.

Nineteenth Sunday of Ordinary Time— Year C

∴⋯⋯⋯⋯∴

Lectio

Luke 12:32–48

Meditatio

> *". . . be prepared. . . ."*

As disciples of Jesus, this command is a priority for us. We can be sure that we are fulfilling God's will if we keep ourselves prepared. But what does it mean? And how can we fulfill it? Jesus tells a story to show us what he means by the command: "Be prepared." Being prepared means that we have such a relationship with the Father—the Master—that when he is absent, we are "vigilant" for his return. When a loved one is absent from home, we long for that person's return. We know exactly when he or she is due back and we make preparations for the homecoming. Life is not the same while our loved one is gone. Something—someone dear to our hearts— is missing.

It's the same with God. While we are on earth, we experience the Father's absence. But in this case, we never know when he will manifest his presence. To be prepared for his coming means to long for it. We live in such a way that we may be able to welcome at any moment the one we long for, the one we know is missing from our lives. Jesus assures us that we have no reason to fear the Father: "Do not be afraid any longer, little flock, for your Father is pleased to give you the kingdom." His story tells us that when the Father finds us waiting for him, *he* will serve *us!*

What a message! The manifestation of the Master's presence is not like that of a taskmaster who comes in and expects everything to be perfectly to his liking, demanding the impossible just because he can. No, he comes like a loved one who has returned home from a journey. On his arrival, he feels so completely at home with us that *he* begins to serve *our* needs.

What are we waiting for?

Oratio

Jesus, thank you for telling us this story about your Father. It makes me feel special to know that your Father looks forward with great longing to my welcoming him, just as I wait for him to manifest his presence. Help me to rid my life of the clutter that keeps me distracted from being prepared to welcome him in my life. Dispel the fear that sometimes moves me to believe that your Father is like a taskmaster who expects me to fulfill his needs. Remind me instead that your Father is more like a loved one who wants to take care of me. Amen.

Contemplatio

Father, I await your return with a welcoming heart.

Monday of the Nineteenth Week
of Ordinary Time

∴ · · · · · · · · · · · ·∴

Lectio

Matthew 17:22–27

Meditatio

> "*. . . that we may not offend them. . . .*"

If you're short on cash, it must be good to go fishing, knowing that your first fly will hook the big one. From this angle, today's Gospel account seems oddly out of sync with Jesus' other miracles, a matter of convenience, a self-serving stunt, like turning stones into bread—which Jesus refused to do. Ironically, both occasions offered him a chance to reaffirm his Sonship, for his sake and ours. The Greek word translated as "subjects" is literally "sons," which Matthew uses to emphasize the Christological meaning of this text. By speaking in the plural, Jesus hints that the word he proclaims is not just about himself. He broadens it to exempt from payment all those born into the kingdom of his Father, children and heirs through the Son, as Paul phrases it (see Rom 8:17).

By paying under protest, does Jesus cave in to the expectations of the status quo? No more than Mary, his mother, denied the unique circumstances of his birth by submitting to ritual purification, which, like the tax, was required by

Jewish law. He will not make a point for others' benefit, then undo it by "offending" them. Like Matthew's Christians, Jesus was an observant Jew. Thus, his privileged position as Son is afforded also to those "children" of the Church, born of Israel into the Father's kingdom.

This episode is not about levying taxes or demanding royalties, though these have their place. Matthew inserted it here most probably to help his Jewish Christian community honor both of its traditions. In our day, Christians with a Jewish background and those in interfaith marriages can relate to that. Actually, we all can. As subjects of the kingdom we are also sons and daughters of the world. We have requirements to fulfill and expectations to meet there as well. With our various commitments, we frequently straddle diverse worlds. Rather than compartmentalize these, how do we integrate them?

Oratio

Jesus, the kings of the earth plotted against you, the Lord's Anointed (see Ps 2:2). You could have stood on your rights as Son. Instead, you chose to give your Church a word of humble love, an example we can follow. Give me your Spirit of wisdom so I can discern how to value and live my convictions, while adapting to our ever-changing times.

Contemplatio

Father, with your openness of spirit, may I live my anointing as your daughter (son).

Tuesday of the Nineteenth Week
of Ordinary Time

∴ · · · · · · · · · · · · ∴

Lectio

Matthew 18:1–5, 10, 12–14

Meditatio

>*". . . will he not . . . go in search of the stray?"*

Why? Why would Jesus search for the stray? He has ninety-nine sheep that stayed in the herd. They are good sheep. This other one is a troublemaker—going away from the herd, getting lost, creating a problem. Just let him go. You still have ninety-nine. It's a little like losing a penny on the street. No matter, a penny doesn't make any difference.

But Jesus, nevertheless, goes after the stray sheep. Why? I believe part of the answer is given to us by Saint Paul. We are the body of Christ. How could Jesus let a part of his body be lost? The more sinful we are, the greater the failures of those in the community, the more tenderly Jesus seeks us out, for we are his body.

What simple and mysterious logic! It is human to be angry at the one who causes problems for the group. It is divine to go search for it as if it were our own body. Recently I broke my arm. So I have had to care for my arm, keeping it still for six weeks, exercising it for twelve weeks, stretching it, lifting it, strengthening it, bending it in all different directions. I do these things because it is part of my body. I need my arm and cannot do without it. Similarly, Jesus seeks out each person (for all of us stray) because we are each part of his body, loved and needed and healed. He cannot do without us. It is a good lesson. The righteous style of my youth gives way to the wise patience of adulthood and to the indomitable love shown to us by Jesus. Love. It is all we are called to, over and over again—love. When the Apostle John was brought out to preach he said only these words, "Love one another."

Oratio

Good Shepherd, I am ashamed of the way I sometimes have thought and spoken about people in the Church because of their beliefs, their behavior, their attitudes, their sins. Teach me to love my brothers and sisters the way I love myself, to cherish them as I care for my own body. I thank you for the times you have come looking for me when I have strayed, and have brought me back.

Contemplatio

I am your body, Jesus. What mystery! What gift!

Wednesday of the Nineteenth Week
of Ordinary Time

$\cdot$············$\cdot$

Lectio

Matthew 18:15–20

Meditatio

"If your brother sins against you, go and tell him his fault. . . ."

This Gospel scene has two characters who call for some attention. First there is the one who sins, and then there is the one who is going to correct the sinner. Attention is often given to the disciple whom Jesus instructs to confront his brother or sister. The reason for correcting the other doesn't come from malice or an attempt to be superior. All of Christ's disciples, including us, are called to act out of love and correct our brother or sister so that he or she can become more like Christ. Correcting someone in matters of faith is a spiritual work of mercy, but that doesn't mean it is easy. Instead, it can be quite difficult and a bit uncomfortable. Yet the person who is being corrected is perhaps in an even more difficult position.

It is always hard to hear the negative side of our actions. When being told that we have hurt someone or that we have acted imprudently, we can respond much like the sinful disciple. We could become defensive and not accept responsibility for the wrongness of what we have done or didn't do (a sin of omission). But we have an alternative. We can choose to receive correction openly and respond graciously. We could wholeheartedly acknowledge the act, ask forgiveness, change our ways, and even thank the person who corrects us. Being a true disciple of Christ requires the ideal characteristics of both the correcting disciple and the corrected disciple. We must act in love toward our brothers and sisters even to the uncomfortable point of correcting them, and we must also acknowledge our humanity and receive correction with humility and gentleness. This humility to both correct and be corrected is a grace given to us by God so that we can be molded more into his image.

Oratio

Jesus Master, I want to be molded more into your image. Fill me with your grace so that I can accept my limitations and act always out of love. When you corrected sinners you did so with gentleness and love. May I follow in your steps when I am called upon to correct and instruct. When I am being corrected, help me to hear you speak to me in the words of my brothers and sisters so that you, through them, may mold me in closer conformity to you. Grant me the grace to act and respond always in gentleness, humility, and love—just as you would do. Amen.

Contemplatio

Jesus, today mold me more and more into your image.

Thursday of the Nineteenth Week of Ordinary Time

⦂· · · · · · · · · · · ·⦂

Lectio

Matthew 18:21–19:1

Meditatio

> " . . . how often must I forgive . . . ?"

While studying abroad, I met a student who came from a culture and religion unfamiliar to me. This student had been offended by someone. In discussing the issue with me, it became clear that the student could not conceive of forgiving that individual. The concept of forgiveness had not been a common belief in that student's religion. The incident confirmed for me that forgiveness is one of the radical concepts of Christianity. That doesn't mean that Christians can *easily* forgive hurts and wrongdoing, especially when they affect us personally. Forgiveness of others and letting go of resentment can be difficult, and it becomes possible through the gift of grace that Christ won for us by his teaching, example, suffering, death, and resurrection.

In today's parable, Jesus tells the story of a man who is forgiven a large debt, and then refuses to forgive another man for a much smaller offense. As we human beings travel through our earthly existence, we bump into one another and cause, or experience, injustice, anger, harsh words and judgments, physical harm, and many other acts and expressions of hostility and pain. Our deeply wounded selves tend to hold on to hurt and resentment. But forgiving and letting go offer unparalleled psychological and spiritual freedom. In a sense, forgiveness can be more important for the injured person than the one who caused the injury. To pardon is to release a cumbersome weight that keeps us imprisoned; to pardon is a divine gift that can restore our distressed and bitter hearts to serenity and joy.

Forgiveness is a process. It may be offered easily, but it may also take us a long time to arrive at the point of pardoning those who wronged us. Sometimes we may only be capable of praying for the person, asking the Divine Master to forgive in our stead until we find in our hearts the freedom of forgiveness.

Oratio

Lord, this business of forgiveness is never easy. When I do not want to forgive a person who hurt me, my distorted thinking likes to believe that I am punishing that person. But in reality, holding on to grievances hurts me even more. Give me, Lord, the grace to forgive, especially when it is difficult. Amen.

Contemplatio

"Our Father, who art in heaven . . . forgive us our trespasses as we forgive those who trespass against us."

Friday of the Nineteenth Week
of Ordinary Time

⟨·············⟩

Lectio

Matthew 19:3–12

Meditatio

> *"Have you not read that from the beginning the Creator
> made them male and female. . . ."*

In the film *Spiderman*, superhero Peter Parker falls in love
with his friend Mary Jane. In an emotionally charged scene,
he tells her that despite his love, he must follow his special
calling. Then he walks away, leaving Mary Jane in tears. In
some way, Parker's choice reflects an understanding of marriage and celibacy, the subject of today's Gospel. But Jesus
brings us to a deeper level. When the Pharisees question him
about divorce, he goes back to the beginning, to Genesis, to
the primeval garden. He tells them that from the beginning,
man and woman were meant to be joined in the "one flesh"
union of marriage. Divorce was not part of that picture, and
Jesus' statement against divorce shocks the apostles. If that's
the case, they object, it's better not to marry! Jesus then
shocks them even more by issuing a call to renounce marriage
for the sake of the kingdom of heaven. To their Jewish ears,
this is unthinkable.

Pope John Paul II used this text in his talks on the theology of the body. He explained how marriage and celibacy are actually two sides of the same coin. They are in reality the same vocation, but lived out in different ways. How so? Love is our vocation, the love expressed in a gift of self to another. In the case of marriage, the love of the spouses binds them together in a gift of self that lasts for life. Their gift is a total gift. In the case of celibacy, the love of a person binds him or her to God in a gift of self that also lasts for life and is a gift shared with others. Both vocations are ways of pouring ourselves out in love for the sake of the beloved. Jesus points out that those who renounce marriage do so "for the sake of the Kingdom of heaven." Celibacy anticipates the resurrection—the heavenly marriage—and is a sign of the future life in the kingdom of God (see Mt 22:30).

Oratio

Jesus, open my eyes to see the beauty of my vocation to love. Help me to make a sincere gift of myself to you and to the people you have put in my life. I pray that married couples may grow in their love, and that those who are consecrated to celibacy for the sake of the kingdom may always witness to the joy that comes from your love.

Contemplatio

Love is my vocation.

Saturday of the Nineteenth Week
of Ordinary Time

∶············∶

Lectio

Matthew 19:13–15

Meditatio

"Let the children come to me. . . ."

A Catholic school in the San Francisco Bay Area has a lovely four-foot statue of a smiling Jesus, sitting down, blessing three children who surround him. Surprisingly, my niece won that statue at a fundraiser and, being seven years old at the time, could not decide what to do with it. As an overzealous aunt, I coaxed her to donate it to her school. It was a good decision. Today, the smiling Jesus surrounded by children sits in a niche in the school's hallway, and he continues to watch over the children who boisterously walk by.

In today's Gospel the disciples become annoyed when parents bring their children to Jesus, as if this is a waste of the Master's time. But Jesus surprises everyone by taking the time to pray with the children and to bless them, by placing his hands on them. Jesus was unique among ancient preachers because he took children seriously and considered them vital members of the kingdom. In fact, he held them up as examples of how to belong to the kingdom of heaven. Children's simplicity, wide-eyed acceptance, total trust, and joyfulness are characteristics that we adults ought to develop in our relationship with God.

Today we need to continue bringing children to Jesus by teaching them about him, their greatest friend, by protecting them, and loving them. Tragically, some children in the world are hungry, abused, neglected, and preyed upon by people with evil intentions. They are forced into various forms of slavery—working at a young age, being used in the sex trade, abducted to fight as soldiers, abandoned to live in the streets. When children experience such unspeakable suffering, Jesus must be weeping, his heart filled with compassion for his little friends. He has a special place in the kingdom of God reserved for these children.

Oratio

Lord Jesus, I ask you to protect and save children from any type of unjust or sinful actions. May families be patient with their lively children. May teachers be good guides to children. May the Church protect children and never hurt them.

Contemplatio

Jesus, Divine Master, hold the children of the world close to your heart!

Twentieth Sunday of Ordinary Time— Year A

:·············:

Lectio

Matthew 15:21–28

Meditatio

"Lord, help me."

The Canaanite woman had already cried out her request, clamoring for Jesus' attention until she got it. Now she kneels at his feet and repeats her plea with simplicity and trust. What could be more disarming than, "Lord, help me"? This simple plea reminds me of my early years of mission. Often, when working with other sisters of my community, I would hear a simple prayer, such as, "Help me, Lord" or "Help me, Jesus." Although I was startled at first, I soon came to appreciate the total sincerity of those prayers said when some difficulty arose. They reflected a sense of personal inadequacy and expressed complete trust. And they worked.

Jesus doesn't respond to the Canaanite woman's request at first. He indicates that it isn't her time yet: she is a Gentile. But her simple trust is wonderful, and who could disregard it for long? At last the Master yields, declaring, "Great is your faith!" This reveals something important: God likes to be trusted and to be asked. We may have difficulty understanding this, because whenever we want to ask someone for help, we weigh the circumstances carefully and perhaps postpone our request, thinking that the person is too busy to be bothered. We forget that, while humans are limited, God is infinite. God has infinite time, as if each of us were the only person in the world.

Nor is God remote, like some busy CEO. In the Book of Proverbs, God's Wisdom (whom the early Christians identified with Jesus) says: "I found delight in the sons of men" (8:31). Jesus came into the world to share our ordinary human life. In the Gospels we find him enjoying human fellowship. Today we can still talk to him in conversational prayer. We can tell the Lord our problems and ask his advice. The answer may not come at that very moment, but perhaps a few hours later. He will answer us in his good time.

Oratio

My Lord and God, I tend to forget that I don't have to tackle difficulties alone—you're ready to enlighten me and give me strength. I want to always remember that you're with me, respecting my freedom and patiently waiting for me to turn to you and ask for help. I'm convinced that you pay attention to me as no one else can and that only you know the answers to all life's problems. You are totally with me. Help me to be with you.

Contemplatio

God has all the time in the world.

Twentieth Sunday of Ordinary Time— Year B

:⋯⋯⋯:

Lectio

John 6:51–58

Meditatio

> *". . . the bread that I will give*
> *is my flesh for the life of the world. . . ."*

I look at Jesus here, hemmed in on all sides by quarreling and questioning from the crowd and from his own followers. I think Jesus must have been acutely aware of the gaze of the crowd, who had pinned their hopes on him and his teaching. Now they watch with disappointment, confusion, and doubt as Jesus repeats in so many different ways that his own flesh and blood are to be eaten, and that whoever eats his flesh and blood will live forever.

In this discourse, Jesus could not have been any clearer. He gives the people the gift of absolute truth, so that they can decide for themselves once and for all who Jesus really is. They can decide what he and his teachings mean for them, and in what way their lives will change from this moment onward. I try to feel what the people felt when they heard Jesus' words, especially that word that he repeated in various ways and that they picked up so quickly: "whoever." This food—his body and blood—is a blessing and grace for everyone. It is not reserved for the literati or the righteous paragons of temple observance.

The food that Jesus will give is food for all, food that comes down from heaven and brings eternal life. Jesus offers a food from heaven that will never run out, accompanying believers through and beyond human history to the kingdom of God, which will never end.

Oratio

After so many years of approaching the sacrament of the Eucharist, I see how the meaning of this sacrament has broadened in my heart. It has moved me beyond the limits set by my thoughts and the catechism that I learned by heart. Jesus, I approach your table with a great and loving hunger now. I am experienced enough with my failures to know that without your presence in my life, I will falter and soon lose my way. Every time I say "amen," I mean it more than the last time I received Communion. Every time I leave Mass with a lighter heart, I know it is you, Jesus, who bears me up.

Contemplatio

Amen.

Twentieth Sunday of Ordinary Time— Year C

⁑············⁑

Lectio

Luke 12:49–53

Meditatio

> *"Do you think that I have come to establish peace on the earth?*
> *No, I tell you, but rather division."*

At first glance, Jesus' words in today's Gospel might startle us. Is Jesus really saying that he came to establish division? I thought he was a man of peace, of communion, and of union, certainly not one of division. So what can he possibly mean? Let's take a closer look.

Jesus begins this discourse by saying to his disciples and to us that he has come to set a fire upon the earth. He ignites this fire through the preaching of his word. When accepted, his word refines and purifies us. Ultimately it transforms us into the persons we are called to be by virtue of our Baptism, that is, other Christs. If this word, however, is rejected, then division, separation, and alienation result, first within ourselves and then even within families. ". . . a father will be divided against his son and a son against his father, a mother against her daughter and a daughter against her mother. . . ."

Yes, the word of God is a point of division. Either we are for Christ or against him; either we are with him or we are apart from him and we take others away from him. The only sure way to peace and communion within ourselves and with one another is through acceptance of this Word who is Christ, the Prince of Peace. We do this in and through faith. So I ask myself: where do I stand? Do I stand with Christ or against him? Do I accept his word that is at times difficult to live, with its many and varied challenges, or do I reject it? My daily actions will show where I stand.

Oratio

Jesus, your word is difficult to live. It constantly challenges me to come out of myself and to direct myself to others, to their needs rather than my own. Your word at times may even separate me from friends and loved ones. Yet I know that ultimately that same word will be a source of communion, union, and peace. Help me to accept your word always. Help me to live it in such a way that I will allow it to transform and change me.

Contemplatio

Jesus, Word of the Father, make me one in you!

Monday of the Twentieth Week of Ordinary Time

∴ · · · · · · · · · · · ∴

Lectio

Matthew 19:16–22

Meditatio

> *"If you wish. . . ."*

The young athlete approached the Olympic trainer. "What do I need to be really good?" Unimpressed, the trainer yawned and said, "You know the routine: eat right, work out daily, see your doctor."

"But I've done that since I could walk! What else?" The coach turned. He sensed something here. With a glint in his eye, he ventured, "If you want to go for the gold, leave everything—family, school, friends, and options. Give away the amateur's gear. Then come, train with me." Later, the youth confessed, "I wanted more, but not *that* much more!"

What do we really want? Paul writes, ". . . the love of money is the root of all evils" (1 Tm 6:10). "Stuff" doesn't make us bad or unhappy, just the attachment does, the clinging for dear life to it. "It" can also be security, position, ability, or friendship. And when these are somehow wrested from our grasp, then come the tantrums. Our relationship to what we value can make or break every other relationship and can lead us into either communion or isolation with respect to others, including Christ. What we want can really impede what we truly want.

A thirty-something woman offered herself to God in prayer one day. Then, realizing the risk, she cried out in her heart, "God, you're always on the take! Can't you leave me, just once, with *something*?" Silently she heard the reply, "I take so you won't be alone." Here is discipleship's payoff: we follow, Jesus accompanies, and this "treasure" lasts forever. This understanding illustrates why this text has traditionally been used to describe "consecrated life"—a radical form of Christian discipleship. Such a life reminds us that willingness to give oneself to Christ makes space within us and among us for a new relationship with him, with our community, with the world, and indeed with ourselves. We are much more than what we own; in fact, we are *other* than what we own. If we want, we can be free to proclaim this Good News with Christ.

Oratio

Teacher, like the young man in today's Gospel, I myself often frame everlasting life in terms of gain and lack. Thank you for inviting me to enter into that life. I know that what I possess tightly possesses me. Give me the courage and trust to face the grasping that prevents me from saying yes. "Many say, 'May we see better times!' But you have given my heart more joy than when grain and wine abound" (Ps 4:7–8).

Contemplatio

"You alone, Lord, make me secure" (Ps 4:9).

Tuesday of the Twentieth Week
of Ordinary Time

⁘ ··········· ⁘

Lectio

Matthew 19:23–30

Meditatio

". . . for God all things are possible. . . ."

The disciples are clearly startled when Jesus tells them that the rich have such a difficult time entering the kingdom of God. It was commonly believed that riches were a sign of God's blessing or favor on the person—"Happy are those who fear the LORD, who greatly delight in God's commands . . . Wealth and riches shall be in their homes; their prosperity shall endure forever" (Ps 112:1, 3). Jesus' saying contradicts a culturally accepted belief. When the disciples hear it, they are probably thinking, "If it's that difficult for someone whom we believe enjoys God's blessing to enter God's kingdom, then *we* don't have a prayer."

It is more difficult for those who are wealthy to trust in God. Their money, or the possessions that their wealth can afford, can become their idol. This idol can easily become the source of their ethics; they are driven to hoard instead of to give, to treat people as a means to increase their wealth, and so forth. Jesus, however, states that the economy of the kingdom of heaven is different. Those who are able to give up material possessions, land, or loved ones for the sake of the kingdom of God will inherit eternal life. They are the ones who populate the kingdom of God. The economy of the kingdom is inverted—those who give away will receive what cannot be purchased: salvation. Therefore, a person's net worth is valued not by what is earned, but by what is given away. This is the economy of the kingdom of God because this is how God acts. The kingdom itself is a gift—given by God. It cannot be purchased; it has no price tag attached. It is impossible for anyone to attain it on one's own because the kingdom of God is *unattainable*. It is a pure gift that, in order to be possessed, must be given and received.

Oratio

Jesus, I am so used to getting what I need by hard work, by setting goals and pursuing them. It is difficult for me to understand any other way of achieving what I desire. Help me to understand, by the gift of your Spirit, that you invite me to accept your kingdom as a gift, not to achieve it as a prize or possession. Enlighten me to know what you are inviting me to give up for the sake of the kingdom. For that act of giving up may open to me the possibility of understanding the economy of your kingdom. Amen.

Contemplatio

Jesus, what is impossible for me is possible for you.

Wednesday of the Twentieth Week of Ordinary Time

⁘ ⋯⋯⋯⋯ ⁘

Lectio

Matthew 20:1–16

Meditatio

> "*. . . my own money. . . .*"

God doesn't have money, and he certainly doesn't *need* it, so this parable must be about something else. Most people would say, "This parable is about rewarding the work we do for God. The people who go into the vineyard early are like good Christians, who support their parish, donate to the food pantry, make honest decisions in their businesses, protect life, and take their kids to church on Sunday." *Well, if that's so*, I ask, *then who are the latecomers who were hired throughout the day?* At this point people begin to squirm a bit. It's hard to point the finger at others and identify them as the latecomers who don't deserve a full day's wages. We might name those whom everyone would agree are either sinners or scoundrels: murderers, terrorists, those involved in child slave traffic or pornography rings. These people make us feel more secure in our place among the laborers who have worked all day in the sun. We, after all, haven't done such awful things. We have a right to heaven and glory.

But somehow we know deep inside that when we point our finger at another, three fingers still point at ourselves. Regardless of how good or bad we feel ourselves or others to be, we are all laborers, "useless servants." If we were wise, we would take on the attitude of the truly evangelical image of the tax collector in the temple: "Forgive me, Lord, I am a sinner." At some moment in our lives God will convict us of our sin, and in the same moment, he will wrap us in an unexpected, incredibly powerful embrace of love. At that moment we will realize that grace is "his own money." He gives it as a gift to everyone, even to me. I will discover then that I am the last laborer hired, and I am still paid for a full day, because there are no wages. There is only the gift of God's love and the merits of Jesus' life, death, and resurrection, which belong to all the sinners he came to save.

Oratio

Jesus, it's easy to convince myself that I'm very good, or despair that I'm very bad. Today I simply want to be who I am: a loved sinner, the lost sheep you searched for and found. It's good to be here.

Contemplatio

Lord Jesus Christ, have mercy on me, a sinner.

Thursday of the Twentieth Week of Ordinary Time

⟨⟩· · · · · · · · · · · ·⟨⟩

Lectio

Matthew 22:1–14

Meditatio

"Come to the feast."

The most obvious application of this Gospel passage is that the grace of salvation is offered to many, but few choose to accept it. The focus is on those who receive an invitation to the wedding celebration. However, as I reflected on this passage, I began to think about it from a different perspective. What about the son of the king whose wedding is the center of this parable? How did he feel that the invited guests rejected the request for their presence at such a memorable occasion? How would I feel? I would feel bewildered, distressed, anguished. It's like the feeling you had in the fifth grade when you gave a valentine to a special friend and didn't receive one back. Or it's like the feeling you have when you are not selected to travel with your boss to a special event but all of your colleagues are. And most difficult of all, it's like the feeling you have when the person you love chooses someone else over you.

Rejection is one of the most devastating experiences of life. Can you imagine what Jesus must feel when we reject his invitations to new life and grace, or when we completely ignore his inspirations? He deeply desires our love, but he leaves us free to accept his invitation to intimacy with him—or not. He would never force us to his wedding banquet; yet he longs for our presence and offers us daily invitations to come to his feast. What if we chose to spend at least fifteen minutes with the Lord each day, speaking to him of our lives, our hopes, our desires, our difficulties, our pains—and listening to his invitations and inspirations? He wants us with him in his presence always. Can we reject such an invitation from the Lord of our lives?

Oratio

Jesus Master, how often have I ignored your invitations, or not even noticed that I was being offered the opportunity to come closer to you. Help me to not reject your invitations to love, but rather to pay attention to your call each day. I also want to encourage the other invited guests—all those I meet—to listen to your invitation and respond to your summons, so that we may celebrate the grace you offer so gratuitously.

Contemplatio

I want to be with you always, Jesus.

Friday of the Twentieth Week
of Ordinary Time

⁚· · · · · · · · · · · · ·⁚

Lectio

Matthew 22:34–40

Meditatio

"You shall love your neighbor as yourself."

The Pharisees have come to Jesus with a question, hoping to trip him up. Their question is not spontaneous, but is meant to pose a dilemma to the Teacher. The scholar of the law who crafted it thinks he has the perfect question, "Teacher, which commandment in the law is the greatest?" Jesus quotes to them the summary statement of the Decalogue from Deuteronomy 6:5, "You shall love the Lord, your God, with all your heart, with all your soul, and with all your mind." He then adds what God said to Moses in the Book of Leviticus, "You shall love your neighbor as yourself" (19:18). Although one is the First Commandment, the other is like it, which is to say they are equal in God's eyes. Not only are all the commandments found in these two, but all the words of the prophets as well. This certainly shakes up the establishment.

Many subsidiary laws that were in effect mitigated the equal status of the command to love one's neighbor wholeheartedly. We know some of these from other Gospel readings we frequently hear, but we read Scripture for our own sake, in order to apply it to our own life. It comes naturally to have a certain focus on ourselves. It's hard to avoid self-love, and in fact, it is critically important to cultivate proper self-love because it sustains us in being: we care for our health, our well-being, our relationships, our education, our jobs, and our families basically because we love ourselves correctly. It is our duty to protect, nourish, and promote ourselves. Jesus says that we should love our neighbors in just the same way, to the same extent, for the same reasons. Would we dare to ask the other famous question here, "Who is my neighbor?" According to Jesus, it is everyone, especially the less desirable. He was himself the exemplar of this command, giving himself completely for all of us on the cross.

Oratio

Dear Lord, you have taught us to be aware of your unconditional love. You have shown us how to focus our own love on you and on our neighbor, your image. Help us to see you in everyone, especially in those who are hardest to accept and most difficult to appreciate. Let us reflect your love on everyone through our kindness and concern. Amen.

Contemplatio

I see and serve you in my neighbor.

Saturday of the Twentieth Week of Ordinary Time

∴ · · · · · · · · · · · · ∴

Lectio

Matthew 23:1–12

Meditatio

> *"They tie up heavy burdens hard to carry and lay them on people's shoulders, but they will not lift a finger to move them."*

In today's Gospel, Jesus challenges the attitude of heart of the Pharisees—and us, too. He asks them to look at the motivations behind what they do, and to seek a deeper interior consistency between their beliefs and their actions. Through the prophets, the God of the Hebrew Scriptures consistently teaches the importance of active love and compassion as a requirement for true faith and worship. In the same way, Jesus teaches the importance of loving our neighbors as ourselves as second only to loving God first, above all else. As Saint John reminds us, "If anyone says, 'I love God,' but hates his brother, he is a liar; for whoever does not love a brother whom he has seen *cannot love God* whom he has not seen" (1 Jn 4:20).

It takes little effort to find people who need our kindness and compassion. Usually, we have no farther to look than our own homes and workplaces! Yet isn't it true that sometimes it is far easier to love the God we don't see than to love the neighbor we do? In these moments the challenge to love becomes concrete, and we come to recognize just how deeply we need God's grace to transform our hearts and lives. Our challenges in living for and with others become the sacramental moments that drive us toward true conversion of heart in Christ. Jesus calls us beyond indifference to a love that shares in the joys, burdens, and sorrows of others. Like Christ, we are called to be attentive, lightening the load of our brothers and sisters through our kindness and love. Sometimes, we can offer only our sincere prayers. Nonetheless, it may be important to ask ourselves, "Is my prayer so sincere that I would be willing to be a part of God's concrete answer to my prayers?" Ultimately, our belief in God has to go beyond external words and be grounded in a deep faith that leads to a readiness to act for the sake of others.

Oratio

Jesus, you are the true Master whose yoke is easy and whose burden is light. You give rest to our souls. I place myself under your yoke, asking you to teach me to walk in your ways. Teach me how to love, and how to cultivate a sincere desire to walk with those who are in need of your tender compassion. May my presence make *you* present—an offering of your tranquillity and rest in a restless, hurting world.

Contemplatio

"Come to me, all you who labor and are burdened, and I will give you rest" (Mt 11:28).

Twenty-First Sunday of Ordinary Time—
Year A

⁞· · · · · · · · · · · · ·⁞

Lectio

Matthew 16:13–20

Meditatio

> *"I will give you the keys to the kingdom of heaven."*

Elsewhere in the Gospels, Jesus' relatives show up on his doorstep because they think he's out of his mind. What would they have done if they had witnessed this conversation between Jesus and the disciples? Jesus affirms Peter's claim that Jesus is the Christ, the *anointed one*, the Son of the living God. (Kings and prophets are anointed, not ordinary folk.) He talks of founding a Church on the "rock" of Peter, of all people! On human terms this is crazy talk. And Jesus goes even further when he entrusts to Peter the "keys to the kingdom of heaven." Peter may have his moments of brilliance, but he also has deep flaws.

"I will give to you. . . ." God is an outlandish giver of gifts. The Master of the Universe entrusted himself, body and soul, into human hands at the annunciation. Mary alone, of us all, honored the gift of incarnation with an unsullied *fiat* throughout her life. God gives himself, body and soul, into our hands in the Eucharist, and the response has been mixed. Sacrilege upon sacrilege have been committed, *and* saints have

been forged and fortified beyond all expectation. Jesus entrusts his authority to bind and loosen into the hands of Peter and by extension, to the other apostles and their successors. In human terms, Jesus is simply too trusting for his own good. During Lent 2000, Cardinal Nguyen Van Thuan gave the spiritual exercises to the papal household. In one of his sermons, he preached on the *defects* of Jesus: Jesus has a horrible memory (of our sins); his math is not accurate and his logic off-balance (the one lost sheep is as valuable as the ninety-nine!); he takes far too many risks; and he clearly doesn't make wise financial calculations. These "defects" come from his great love—that gives all, trusts all, and empowers all.

Oratio

Lord, your thoughts are beyond my thoughts, your ways are beyond my ways. I remain humbled before your gifts given to Peter and his successors. I am astounded at the graces poured out on the whole Church. And Jesus, where can I begin to describe the treasures you've entrusted to me? My God, you are an absurdly lavish giver! You make us in your image and likeness, and we find our true happiness in following your lead. Give me a generous heart after the pattern of your own foolishly generous heart.

Contemplatio

I remain humbled before your gifts.

Twenty-First Sunday of Ordinary Time—
Year B

⋮⋯⋯⋯⋯⋮

Lectio

John 6:60–69

Meditatio

"Master, to whom shall we go? . . . you are the Holy One of God."

Just as in the Synoptic Gospels in which Peter proclaims Jesus as the Messiah, in John's Gospel he proclaims Jesus as the Holy One of God, who has the words of eternal life. Peter has come to believe in Jesus' divine origin. This must have been a bittersweet moment for Jesus. It is bitter because many of his disciples refuse to accept his teaching on the Eucharist and leave him, and also because Jesus knows that one of the Twelve will betray him. But it is sweet because Peter, in the name of his companions, professes belief that the Master was sent by God.

I wonder if Peter was receptive to divine illumination because of his love for the Master. I wonder, too, whether he later mulled over what he had impulsively exclaimed and made some connection with the Scriptures. For example, in Deuteronomy, God promises to send a prophet "like Moses" to whom the people would listen (see Dt 18:15–19). Isaiah promises that someday Israel's teacher would no longer hide himself; people would see him with their own eyes (see Is 30:20). The wisdom books (Proverbs, Wisdom, and Sirach) tell of God's personified Wisdom, described as coming forth from the Most High to carry out his bidding in the world. If Peter and the others didn't recall those passages then, they certainly would in the future.

We, too, profess that Jesus is the Holy One of God, sent into the world with the words of eternal life. We meditate on these words and try to live by them. How can we help friends and family members find the light and strength that we ourselves draw from the Gospel?

Oratio

Jesus, Divine Master, you are the prophet foretold in Deuteronomy, the teacher prophesied by Isaiah; you are the Wisdom of God described in the sapiential writings. You are the Word who was made flesh and lived among us, full of grace and truth. I draw light and strength from your teachings. I want to lead others to you. I'm especially thinking of *(name whomever you particularly want to bring closer to Jesus)*. Enlighten me about this. You can do all things. As you have done before in my life, arrange the circumstances to make this all work out. I want to be your agent, your instrument. Divine Master, show me the way.

Contemplatio

"You have the words of eternal life."

Twenty-First Sunday of Ordinary Time—
Year C

∴ ⋯⋯⋯⋯ ∴

Lectio

Luke 13:22–30

Meditatio

"After the master of the house has arisen and locked the door, then you will stand outside knocking and saying, 'Lord, open the door for us.'"

Luke's thirteenth chapter is about the call to conversion and repentance, which this parable stresses. A key word in the above verse is *after*. The one who is standing outside and knocking is, in fact, admitting that he or she doesn't really know the Lord. The person has eaten and drunk with Jesus, and even heard him preach—so the question arises, why is the person outside? One who has heard the Lord preach cannot claim to be ignorant about what to do. After hearing the call to repentance and conversion, the only reason to remain outside is a failure to take action. In other words, the person has procrastinated.

How many times have we put off until tomorrow the difficult things we would rather not do? Probably those instances are too numerous to count. We pray with Scripture, we have dined with the Lord at the Eucharist, we have heard him preaching through our priests and bishops. He clearly invites us to repentance and conversion, yet how often we put it off. Jesus invites us to change through the questions he puts in our hearts. Am I being selfish with my time? Do I hold myself above or beneath others? Do I love God with my whole heart, soul, and mind, and love his people as I should love myself? Such questions are invitations to change and to express sorrow for past injustices. We are called not to stand outside, but to enter through the door today by being open to inner conversion. With the invitation, Jesus gives us the grace to repent and convert. He calls to us, "Do not delay; do not procrastinate. Look on the face of Love and enter through the door. Don't stay outside any longer, but be grateful for God's mercy and goodness!"

Oratio

Lord, you have invited me this day to walk through the door of love and service, and my heart is stirring in response. Gently you have questioned and prodded me to reflect on my actions, and I thank you for loving me enough to do that. I do not want to put off any longer the change to which you are inviting me. I want to become more like you, to love as you love, to serve others as you would have me serve them. Help me to respond today to the grace you have given me to act upon your invitation. Amen.

Contemplatio

". . . now is a very acceptable time; behold, now is the day of salvation" (2 Cor 6:2).

Monday of the Twenty-First Week
of Ordinary Time

⁘ ⋯⋯⋯ ⁘

Lectio

Matthew 23:13–22

Meditatio

"Woe to you. . . ."

Jesus speaks powerful words to some scribes and Pharisees in today's Gospel. We can imagine the emotion as he cries out, "Woe to you!" What we might forget is that Jesus loves these people whose practices he condemns. He loves them so much that he willingly gives up his life so they can be redeemed. The rebukes we hear in today's Gospel are made in love and for love. We don't know if any of the listeners changed as a result of Jesus' words and love. *We*, however, can come to a deeper realization of God's love for us and respond to it. God loves us just as he did these scribes and Pharisees—with an unconditional, enduring love—no matter what. It is important that we know this within ourselves. This knowledge is usually not a feeling, but rather an ever-deepening belief. When life goes smoothly, it may seem easy to believe in God's love. However, our belief deepens and becomes more life-giving when we are struggling with challenges, darkness, or pain. Such moments are opportunities to turn to God and honestly express our feelings, fears, and needs.

Sometimes God seems silent, but we continue to speak and listen. Gradually we become aware that God is our faithful companion who provides us with grace and strength. We experience God's love for us.

When we believe that nothing will cause God to stop loving us, we are encouraged in our efforts to become more holy. We have the courage and grace to turn to God for forgiveness whenever we sin or give in to our weaknesses. As we continue reflecting on God's love, we can make another application: God loves *everyone* unconditionally: everyone with whom I live and work, everyone I meet each day. Aware of this, I therefore seek to accept others as they are, treating them with respect and love, forgiving and asking forgiveness. When we know that God loves us, our own love grows and expands.

Oratio

Beloved God, it is sometimes hard to believe how much you love me. Thank you for loving me no matter what I do or how I fail! Give me the grace to trust your love. Help me to turn to you for strength, comfort, and grace. Whenever I sin, enable me to turn to you for forgiveness. The more I accept your love for me, the more I am able to love others. It is sometimes so difficult to accept others as they are. Please give me the grace to gradually love as you do. I ask this in Jesus' name. Amen.

Contemplatio

I trust in your love for me.

Tuesday of the Twenty-First Week of Ordinary Time

⁝⋯⋯⋯⋯⋯⁝

Lectio

Matthew 23:23–26

Meditatio

> *". . . judgment and mercy and fidelity."*

Jesus is still at it in today's Gospel, taking aim at the practices of the scribes and Pharisees (but not at their teachings). Like the prophets of old, Jesus offers a stinging critique of practices that were not wrong in themselves but which were carried to such an extreme that their meaning was lost. He wants to bring the scribes and Pharisees into full conformity with God's will, which is never simply an external practice.

The passage could almost be part of the Sermon on the Mount with its emphasis on seeking God's kingship and justice (see Mt 6:33). It is the perennial temptation of devout people to replace these by overemphasizing externals, the way Jesus teasingly portrays the scribes and Pharisees as doing: not satisfied with paying tithes on their *crops* as the Law requires, they even measure out 10 percent of the tiny seeds of garden herbs. (Whole cumin seeds are the size of caraway or fennel seeds.) Such scrupulosity can cause one to lose track of what today's Gospel sums up as "judgment and mercy and fidelity."

Why the Pharisees make such distinctions is easy enough to understand: It's much easier to focus on things that are more within our reach, and external things are under our control. After all, justice, mercy, and fidelity are attributes of *God!* Tithes, even of herbs, are at least within our reach. Saint Paul called this seeking "a justice of one's own" (see Phil 3:9). It means, Paul hints, keeping oneself outside the realm of grace.

Oratio

Centuries later, Lord, it is still a temptation for me to distract myself with rules and practices to such an extent that I forget to honor you! How convenient for me when that "higher" duty is also more manageable, more within reach, more clearly and cleanly defined, and even measurable. The neater the outcomes, the easier it is for me to feel confident that I have "fulfilled all righteousness" (see Mt 3:15). Invoking a "higher" law or value may even be a ruse I set up for myself, to protect me from responding freely and fully when faced with human need. Jesus, you spoke plainly but mercifully to the scribes and Pharisees. Break through my self-deceptions, too, so that I keep "judgment and mercy and fidelity" as the central criteria that guide my choices and priorities.

Contemplatio

Seek first God's kingdom and justice (see Mt 6:33).

Wednesday of the Twenty-First Week of Ordinary Time

⟨·············⟩

Lectio

Matthew 23:27–32

Meditatio

" . . . on the outside you appear righteous, but inside you are filled with hypocrisy and evildoing."

Jesus sounds harsh in his rebuke of the scribes and Pharisees in this Gospel. It might sound as if he is rebuking some terrible sinners. But the people of Jesus' day did not consider the scribes and Pharisees as sinners, as they did the tax collectors and prostitutes. The scribes were religious professionals—something like priests and religious today. And the Pharisees were laymen who were trying to live their faith fully, beyond the bare minimum—something like Catholics who go to daily Mass. Jesus' rebuke is also addressed to *us*. On the outside we may look like good and holy people. Jesus isn't saying that we shouldn't. It's praiseworthy to raise our children conscientiously; dress modestly; and give of our time, talent, and treasure in charitable works. But what is on the *inside*? What is in our hearts? Jesus comes back to this many times in the Gospel.

"Evildoing" is a strong word. How do we do evil "inside"? Even if our actions—the things we do—are good on the surface, in our hearts we can have thoughts and motives that are less than good. For example, we might be judgmental of others, considering ourselves better because of our good actions. Or we might envy others, hoping they will fail or that something negative about them will come to light so we will appear better by comparison. The possibilities are endless! It's important to remember that temptation is not the same as evildoing. We might have the temptation to envy someone—in other words, the feeling comes to us, unbidden. But if we are truthful with ourselves, we will know whether we resisted that thought or gave it room in our heart. Jesus is pointing out that we need to keep careful watch over our hearts, so that our actions might flow out of a good heart as we follow him.

Oratio

Jesus, give me the courage and honesty to look into my own heart and find the hypocrisy and evildoing that I have allowed to enter but which I want to clear out of my life. I know I must do this interior work regularly because, despite my best intentions, I allow certain things to creep back in. Jesus, my heart is for you. Help me keep it free and loving, that you may dwell there.

Contemplatio

My heart belongs to you, Lord.

Thursday of the Twenty-First Week of Ordinary Time

:·············:

Lectio

Matthew 24:42–51

Meditatio

"Stay awake!"

The Greek word translated as "stay awake" indicates a constant vigil. Monks of the Eastern tradition would keep vigil through the night in prayer, standing toward the rising sun, in a gesture symbolic of the stance all creatures should have as we await the final return of the Son of God. We are more familiar with vigils at the bedside of the sick or dying. We keep vigil with others, comforting them with our presence, awaiting a turn for the better or a dying person's last breath. We are all too familiar with waiting, but sometimes our waiting is not like watching in constant vigil. We wait for conflicts to end or babies to be born. We wait for pay increases, good weather, or Christmas to arrive. We wait in checkout lines, restaurants, to receive the Eucharist. We spend much of our life waiting. And the waiting often frustrates and annoys us, breaks our hearts, or leads to boredom.

Today's Gospel might seem distant to us with its stories of thieves breaking into a house, servants and masters, and food distribution. A deeper level of meaning can be found here, however. We all are waiting, on many levels, for many things. We wait for the passing of time and the end of things over which we have no control. We wait for the second coming of the Son of Man. All this frustrating or boring "waiting time" can be transformed into "vigil time." By keeping constant vigil we wait in a spirit of prayer, expecting God's loving providence for us now and always. In keeping vigil we support and comfort others, being present and attentive to their every need. Living life as a constant vigil, we have a hushed anticipation that the glory of the Resurrected One shines over the darkness of this world's sorrow and pain.

Oratio

Our Father, who art in heaven, hallowed be thy name. Thy kingdom come. From this moment forward I will strain to see your face everywhere I go. I will watch for you in my neighbor, in my church, in my place of work. I will keep vigil in prayer in the silence of my heart and in the beauty of the community at Eucharist. Maranatha!

Contemplatio

Come, Lord Jesus, come.

Friday of the Twenty-First Week of Ordinary Time

∵ · · · · · · · · · · · · ∵

Lectio

Matthew 25:1–13

Meditatio

"Therefore, stay awake, for you know neither the day nor the hour."

Today's parable is given to us in the context of a wedding feast. In Jesus' time, bridesmaids holding oil lamps would form a procession to welcome the bride and bridegroom outside the village, then lead them safely through the darkness to the bridegroom's house. Bridesmaids enhanced the beauty and solemnity of the wedding. The ten virgins in this parable all fall asleep as they wait for the wedding company to arrive. Not only did the foolish maidens fail to anticipate the groom's delay, but they also neglected to bring enough oil, then fell asleep instead of buying some. They disregarded their duty as servants because they were lazy and careless. To be without oil is a sign of their infidelity. Had the wise virgins shared their oil with them, there would not have been enough to welcome and lead the wedding party through the city streets to the bridegroom's feast.

Oil and light are powerful symbols in the Judaeo-Christian heritage. Oil symbolizes the good deeds necessary to keep lamps burning brightly. Good deeds belong to the person who performs them; that is why the wise virgins could not share the "oil" of their deeds with the foolish virgins. Oil also symbolizes God's blessings poured out in the sacramental signs of Baptism, Confirmation, Holy Orders, and the Anointing of the Sick. The lamp is a sign of a life of integrity. The message of today's parable is clear: the wise disciples are those who are prepared for the Lord's coming. The parable of the ten virgins teaches us not to live self-centered lives that are focused on the pursuit of comfort, but to watch for the Lord's coming. The Father arranged the marriage of Jesus, the bridegroom who came to save humanity. The bridegroom's delay stands for the delay of Jesus' second coming. The ten virgins signify the Christian community, and the closing of the door represents the Last Judgment. This parable warns us to be well prepared for the Lord's coming, because we do not know when that will be.

Oratio

Jesus, you long for union with every man and woman. May my heart be like a burning lamp that waits to welcome you when you come. Help me to live a life rich in loving deeds, attentive to lightening the burdens of others. Make me watchful and ready to be a light to help guide others to you, the Light of the World.

Contemplatio

I wait with burning lamp for you, Lord.

Saturday of the Twenty-First Week of Ordinary Time

∴ · · · · · · · · · · · · ∴

Lectio

Matthew 25:14–30

Meditatio

> *"Come, share your Master's joy."*

As you read this parable, notice the great differences between the relationships that the three servants have with their master. On the one hand, the servant who receives the one talent is operating out of a relationship of fear: He says, "Master, I knew you were a demanding person . . . so out of fear. . . ." By contrast, the master praises the other two servants for their faithfulness and invites them into a deeper experience of joy with him. Faithfulness and sharing another's joy can only happen in the context of a good relationship, rooted in mutual trust and concrete experiences of shared love. Jesus' parable reveals that the master's focus is not primarily on using his servants for his own gain, but on inviting them into a closer relationship with him and a deeper sharing in his joy. The responsibilities the master gives the faithful servants and their obedience in carrying them out flow from their growing love and trust for one another.

This parable gives us an opportunity to pause and reflect on the quality of our relationships with God and our neighbors. We want our relationships with others to be based on authentic and transparent love, rooted in our relationship with God. We don't want them to be based on false masks or on a desire to gain something from the other. The Lord invites each of us to place our relationship with him at the center of all our interactions, words, and choices. Then, like the two faithful servants, we can move away from fear and know the joy of living in a good relationship with the Lord and the other people in our lives.

Oratio

Jesus Master, help me to become more aware of the deep motivations that guide the choices I make. Help me to look honestly with you at all the relationships that are a part of my life, and above all, my relationship with you. I want to move away from forming relationships out of fear, or a desire to avoid punishment and failure. Help me to deeply receive your love for me so your love can grow in me and bear fruit in my relationships with others.

Contemplatio

"Do not be afraid; you are worth more than many sparrows" (Mt 10:31).

Twenty-Second Sunday of Ordinary Time—Year A

⋮ · · · · · · · · · · · · ⋮

Lectio

Matthew 16:21–27

Meditatio

> *"Jesus began to show his disciples that he must go to Jerusalem and suffer greatly. . . ."*

Suffering is one of those existential realities that defy our human understanding. We try to reason it away, but find that it becomes more of a mystery. We don't want to suffer, and, even more, we don't want to see our loved ones suffer. Our natural response is to want to fix the situation and to alleviate the pain. Even if we try, very quickly we recognize our feebleness and inadequacy. We are anguished over any affliction. When Peter hears Jesus predict that he will suffer greatly and be put to death, Peter can't bear it. Frantically, he reasons that he must stop it from happening. "God forbid, Lord! No such thing shall ever happen to you!" Suffering is unacceptable, especially for the Messiah. This is the human response. Stop the suffering. End the pain. Avoid and prevent.

Jesus responds to Peter harshly and unexpectedly. "Get behind me, Satan! . . . You are thinking not as God does, but as human beings do." Yes, Peter is thinking as a human being:

remove and avoid what causes suffering. Any of us probably would have said the same thing. So, how does God think of suffering? Suffering is not an end in itself. God doesn't wish us to suffer and be in pain. But we can learn something from our suffering that we would not otherwise learn if we never experience this dumbfounding reality. We learn acceptance. We learn surrender. We learn that we are not almighty. Suffering humbles us and leads us to rely on God, who alone is Master of our lives. We can either think of suffering as something to avoid, or we can let it become an opportunity to learn that we are not in control of our lives. We can surrender our hold on life so that we can truly be free.

Oratio

Master, some things in my life are causing me to suffer right now. Help me to understand in what areas I should not be trying to avoid pain. Instead, teach me to look at it as a means for surrendering, so that I may allow you to work your miracles in me. Help me to let go of my need to control so that I might trust more deeply in you.

Contemplatio

You are Lord of my life.

Twenty-Second Sunday of Ordinary Time— Year B

⁝·············⁝

Lectio

Mark 7:1–8, 14–15, 21–23

Meditatio

> "... their hearts are far from me."

The Pharisees and their predecessors had formulated many rules, which they felt would help people keep God's law. But the letter of the law can become everything, and its spirit nothing. Jesus challenges the Pharisees to recognize that they have gone off track. "This people honors me with their lips," he quotes, "but their hearts are far from me." Probably *Jesus'* purpose is to recall the Pharisees to their duty—reminding them that interior dispositions have more value than pious exterior actions. *Mark's* purpose may have been different, since he seems to have written for the Christian community in Rome, which was partly Gentile. Mark may have been chiefly interested in what Jesus said about Jewish dietary laws.

And what is the *Church's* purpose in presenting this Gospel reading to us today? Although we might have the attitudes that Jesus warned against—exterior piety, interior vice—this Gospel could have another message for us: Where *is* our heart? Where do our thoughts roam? What do we do for enjoyment, and how often? Are we addicted to some substance or activity? A person can be addicted to far more than tobacco, drugs, and alcohol. Other addictions, for example, could be greed, envy, and other vices mentioned in this Gospel passage, as well as certain foods or favorite types of novels, films, TV shows, and other forms of entertainment. Not all diversions are addictions, but if they interfere with our responsibilities—the duties of our state in life—they become problematic. In all this, how much room is there for God? It's a challenge to keep God in the forefront of our lives. The First Commandment states: "you shall not have other gods besides me" (Ex 20:3). Following this commandment can be difficult, because we don't see God. Praying, reading Scripture and spiritual books, and contemplating nature or sacred images are all means of keeping in touch with God, so that he may never find our hearts "far from" him.

Oratio

Lord God, I want to give you the place in my life that you deserve and carry out the duties of my state for love of you. Help me to overcome any addictions or diversions that interfere with my relationship with you or with my other responsibilities. You are the reason and goal of my existence. Inspire me to stay close to you. I want to be with you always.

Contemplatio

Lord, help me to keep in touch.

Twenty-Second Sunday of Ordinary Time— Year C

∴ · · · · · · · · · · · · ∴

Lectio

Luke 14:1, 7–14

Meditatio

". . . blessed indeed will you be. . . ."

Miss Manners would have been appalled at today's Gospel scene. Unlike Jesus, she would have advised every "Gentle Reader" to wait to be seated by the host. She may have remarked that a guest list does not commonly include "the poor, the crippled, the lame, the blind," and that Jesus was rude to upbraid his host! But Jesus' wisdom transcends mere etiquette, even if it has profound social implications. His eyes are fixed on the Father, who "causes rain to fall on the just and the unjust" (Mt 5:45), and who beckons everyone from "the streets and alleys of the town" to join in the wedding reception for his Son (see Lk 14:15ff.). Imagine a world where everyone looks out for one another, not only from a sense of justice, but also out of humble love. It's possible only if we recognize how we ourselves have been received.

The scene also recalls the table Jesus spreads in his words "spoken publicly to the world" (Jn 18:20) and in his body offered "to gather into one the dispersed children of God" (Jn 11:52). It is a table he spreads sacramentally even now "on behalf of many" (Mt 26:28). The Eucharist is the sign of the heavenly banquet where everyone, without exception, dines in communion with Christ and one another. Today's teaching foreshadows his ultimate self-gift, presenting him as an inviting example: ". . . as I have done for you, you should also do" (Jn 13:15). The promise? We will be "repaid at the resurrection of the righteous." The beauty of Christ's teaching here and throughout the Gospel is that as we try to make this world a better place, the people we become in the process never die. This is not only reward, but an uninterrupted continuum made gloriously complete in the resurrection of these bodies that have welcomed one another.

Oratio

Master, sometimes when I look at our world, I get discouraged. If only we *all* followed your teaching. Many people don't care, though. Others care, but fall short.

What's that? Forgive as I'm forgiven? Don't judge, and I won't be judged? Oh, right. How many of us may have to relinquish our presumed places of honor in the kingdom to make way for those who've wronged you, blindsided us, repented (even poorly), and hobbled in making amends? Actually, I do all those things. As I humbly accept them, open me more to receive the grace that can transform the world.

Contemplatio

"My reward is with the Lord, my recompense is with my God" (Is 49:4).

Monday of the Twenty-Second Week of Ordinary Time

:⋯⋯⋯:

Lectio

Luke 4:16–30

Meditatio

> *"Today this scripture passage is fulfilled. . . ."*

Luke tells us the people's response as Jesus developed his homily: They "were amazed at the gracious words *that came from his mouth.*" Luke isn't just stating the obvious. In this passage Jesus is claiming his messianic role. Luke's words refer to Psalm 45, a messianic psalm known as the "royal wedding song." The psalmist says to "the king" that "fair speech has graced your lips." That brings to mind Luke 6:45 ("from the fullness of the heart, the mouth speaks") and even the prologue of John, "from his fullness we have all received, grace in place of grace" (Jn 1:16), which leads to John's own conclusion (and a very apt summing up of today's Gospel): "No one has ever seen God. The only Son, God, who is at the Father's side, has revealed him" (Jn 1:18).

Saint Thérèse of Lisieux wrote that she desired to learn Greek so that she could read the New Testament without the intermediary of translation: to receive the word right from the mouth of God. When I read this passage from Luke, I want to learn Hebrew, so I can read the same words that Jesus read that Sabbath in Nazareth. He looked up from the text that day and announced that those words, already so ancient and revered in his day, were fulfilled.

Actually, my desire is superficial compared to what the Lord offers in today's Gospel passage. He isn't merely suggesting that I find communion with him by learning to read the same language he read: he offers me profound communion with him *in the fulfillment of the prophecy*! He offers to let those Scriptures be fulfilled today, as he lives in me to heal the brokenhearted, "to proclaim liberty to captives and recovery of sight to the blind . . . to proclaim a year acceptable to the Lord." And I don't have to learn Hebrew for that!

Oratio

Lord, that crowd in the Nazareth synagogue was amazed by the fullness of grace and truth that came from your lips as you made God known to them in the Scriptures and in yourself. But it is not enough that the Scriptures were fulfilled in your human life: you want them to be continuously fulfilled in your Mystical Body. You want me to share in this grace today. Open my mind and heart to the opportunities *today* to bring sight to the blind (and receive sight myself), freedom to captives (and to accept the challenges of interior freedom myself), and healing to the brokenhearted (as I also allow my heart to be touched and made new).

Contemplatio

Today the Scriptures are fulfilled. . . .

Tuesday of the Twenty-Second Week
of Ordinary Time

⁘ · · · · · · · · · · · · ⁘

Lectio

Luke 4:31–37

Meditatio

> " . . . *they were astonished at his teaching.* . . ."

Luke's Gospel begins with narratives about God sending messages to people and their response. God sends the Angel Gabriel first to Zechariah to announce the birth of John the Baptist, and then to Mary to announce the birth of Jesus. In each case the birth would be miraculous. Elizabeth, Zechariah's wife, was past childbearing age, and Mary would conceive as a virgin. The doubtful Zechariah demanded proof: "How shall I know this?" (Lk 1:18). The believing Mary asked for information: "How can this be, since I have no relations with a man?" (Lk 1:34). Zechariah was punished for not believing the angel's word. Mary, instead, was told that she would be overshadowed by the Holy Spirit and the child to be born would be the Son of God. Then she declared herself God's servant and gave herself over completely to all that God had planned.

Throughout Luke and Acts we see this theme repeatedly: the divine announcement or teaching, and the human response. The angels call poor shepherds to come see the newborn Jesus and then to tell others about it. Simeon and Anna follow inspiration and come to the temple when Mary and Joseph bring Jesus there. Simeon tells Mary that Jesus would be the cause for the rise and the downfall of many in Israel—depending on their response. Luke presents Mary as the model of all who hear God's word: she *ponders* everything in her heart and she *follows* the path marked out before her. In today's Gospel we witness the first healing after Jesus began his public ministry. The listeners are "astonished." After the healing they are "amazed." Since news of him spread everywhere, we can assume the people talked to their neighbors about what they had witnessed. To move from simply being amazed—informed, entertained, intrigued, curious, interested—to being a completely dedicated servant of the Lord, we must pass over a bridge. That bridge is "pondering in one's heart."

Oratio

Mary, teach me to ponder. I have so little time and so much to do. Did you have a lot of time to think and meditate and pray? As a new mother, probably not. Teach me how to ponder as I go and to learn from everything. Make me sensitive to God's voice and obedient to his will.

Contemplatio

O God, my God, I open myself to your word.

Wednesday of the Twenty-Second Week of Ordinary Time

∴ · · · · · · · · · · · · ∴

Lectio

Luke 4:38–44

Meditatio

"The crowds went looking for him. . . ."

Today they're looking for you, Jesus, to try "to prevent [you] from leaving them." A dozen verses earlier (in Monday's Gospel reading) the crowd was so incensed that they were going to throw you headlong off a cliff. That was Nazareth; now you're back in Capernaum and they're hanging on your every word. Tomorrow you'll overwhelm Peter, who will ask you to leave him because you're out of his league and he knows it. On Friday the Pharisees are going to start sticking you under the microscope. They love you. They hate you. They love you. They hate you . . . . And there you are in the midst of contradictory expectations and reactions, holding fast to the Father's plan of revealing the good news of the Kingdom of God.

Where am I in this Gospel narrative? I, too come looking for Jesus. Here I am making space to meditate on his Word given to us in the liturgy. What am I really doing here? What do I desire from this encounter? The crowd in today's Gospel go looking for Jesus to prevent him from leaving their town.

They're almost on the right track. After all, he cured their sick and expelled demons. Who wouldn't want to have someone like that around? The problem is that the good people of Capernaum are just looking for a village miracle worker, and Jesus knows that his vocation is to be Savior of the whole world.

Throughout the Gospels, Jesus never loses track of his primary vocation. He is the Son of the Father—he *is* the revelation of God's goodness and truth in the world. He is self-giving Love that heals and restores fallen humanity into relationship with God, even at the price of his own blood. The crowds go looking for Jesus only because he came from heaven to look for God's lost and wandering people in the first place.

Oratio

Here I am, Lord. I am looking for you because you came looking for me first. Lord, open my heart and my eyes to see my vocation in life from your perspective. Purify my understanding of our relationship. Lord, throughout the Gospels you followed the Father's plan for you in the midst of wildly divergent reactions and expectations from those around you. I want to be like that. Help me to see my part in God's loving plan of salvation, and to stay true to it in the midst of this day's joys and challenges.

Contemplatio

Why do I go looking for Jesus?

Thursday of the Twenty-Second Week of Ordinary Time

⁝··········⁝

Lectio

Luke 5:1–11

Meditatio

> " . . . at your command I will lower the nets."

It must have been quite a shock for Peter to have his workaday routine upset by this itinerant rabbi. Peter and his partners had been out on the lake all night, disappointed because they weren't able to catch any fish. In preparation for their next excursion, they are mending their nets. Then along comes Jesus—a traveling rabbi. Once he has finished doing what a rabbi does, he turns to tell the fishermen to go back out for a catch. Rather than telling the rabbi that this is the worst possible time to go fishing, that they need to prepare their nets, and that he and his men are looking forward to going home and relaxing, Peter follows the rabbi's command.

What's really happening here? Jesus is asking Peter to go against the first commandment of human existence: to play it safe. He invites Peter to move beyond the safety of human and physical limitation into the realm of the unknown. The overwhelming success of this adventure and the physical presence of this rabbi overwhelm Peter with the hidden reality of God's presence. When we allow God in and experience what happens when the divine interacts with the human, we experience an overwhelming sense of closeness. Even though we may be uncomfortable with that nearness and the incredible realization that God is so close to us, the experience leaves us wanting more.

Each of us is invited to "put out into deep water"—to stop living according to the limitations of our human expectations. When we let go of whatever moors us to the physical plane of reality, and allow ourselves to follow God's invitation toward the spiritual ideals to which God beckons us, we will be surprised at the overwhelming sense of fulfillment that we discover.

Oratio

Jesus, I feel the tug in my heart urging me to embrace a higher ideal. Yet I make excuses for staying within the confines of my weakness and shortsightedness. I fear what I don't know and can't see. In this Gospel passage, you beckon to me to rely on you when I know I am called to pursue what seems to be beyond human limitation. Help me to trust your presence; help me remember that you see what I cannot see. I am confident that with you guiding me, I will find rest. Amen.

Contemplatio

I have nothing to fear, for God is with me.

Friday of the Twenty-Second Week of Ordinary Time

∴ · · · · · · · · · · · · ∵

Lectio

Luke 5:33–39

Meditatio

> " . . . *no one pours new wine into old wineskins.*"

Early in this passage Jesus explains why his disciples don't fast: the Bridegroom is at the feast with the bride (God's people). Something new and joyful is taking place, and it's incompatible with the practice of fasting.

To this explanation, the evangelist attaches two of Jesus' parables about new versus old: If sewn onto an old garment, an unshrunken patch will make a large rent. If used to fill up old wineskins, new wine will burst the skins. The message is "new with the new" and "old with the old."

At one point, I found this puzzling. How does one move from old to new if the two are incompatible? In reflecting, I noted that the two parables really concern attitudes, which are often easier to change than processes or procedures. If a person's attitude can change, the new *is* possible. And, of course, that was what happened in the early Church. Some Jewish Christians, like Paul, were able to change their outlook in order to admit Gentiles into the Church without obliging them to embrace Judaism first.

I think these parables have much to teach us today. It's good to be open to the new. I don't mean that we should accept everything that's trendy. If we can look at the new with an open mind, we can decide whether it's worthwhile to embrace it. Not to move at all is to stagnate. John Henry Newman wrote that living involves changing, and becoming perfect means changing often. Even though in ordinary life old wine is better, at Cana the new wine that Jesus produced was the *best*.

Oratio

Holy Spirit, help me to evaluate anything new that comes my way and to decide whether it's for me. I want to change for the better. Help me to see what I can improve in my life: Replace an unhealthy habit with a new and wholesome one? Give new life to a foundering relationship? Enhance my prayer life with a new way of praying? Take a new approach to the sacrament of Reconciliation? Inject new fervor into my Mass participation? Guide me, Holy Spirit, in true interior renewal.

Contemplatio

Jesus' new wine is the best.

Saturday of the Twenty-Second Week
of Ordinary Time

:············:

Lectio

Luke 6:1–5

Meditatio

"Have you not read . . . ?"

Sometimes holy people can scandalize us. When David went into the Temple and took the consecrated "bread of offering" as food for himself and his warriors, wasn't he acting like a law unto himself? Why, then, is Jesus pointing to him as an example?

It's all in how you read the story. As Saint Paul said, these things were written for our instruction (see I Cor 10:11), but the simple ability to read is not very helpful if we are unable to interpret the text. In the matter of the temple bread, David broke more than the letter of the Law or the later, protective wall of observances around it. It is as if David was reading something between the lines that the rest of us, like the Pharisees, couldn't even see. Jesus implies that this is why David's example is still valid and ought to be applied.

David was a "man after [God's] own heart" (I Sam 13:14; see Acts 13:22). Like many saints after him, he had almost an intuitive sense of God's purpose; a kind of communion of understanding and of will. And so, faced with his own hunger and that of his band, David acted as "lord" of the Temple bread, redirecting its purpose.

In referring to David, Jesus was beginning a Copernican revolution of his own: it is not the Sabbath that is the sun around which the Law circles. It is he himself, Jesus, who is the Lord of the Sabbath, the center of gravity around which the Sabbath turns. When the Lord of the Sabbath is present, there is no need for others to "enforce" the Sabbath.

Oratio

Lord, this story reminds me of the experiences of some of the saints, like Saint Francis of Assisi, Saint Ignatius of Loyola, or Saint Teresa of Avila. They responded to you in radical ways, so much more intense than what people had come to see as "normal," that these saints were themselves thought to be suspect in their orthodoxy (if not just plain crazy). Saint Paul said "the spiritual person . . . is not subject to judgment by anyone" (I Cor 2:15). Who would have the criteria by which to judge people guided by the Holy Spirit? That is the ultimate interpretive key for Scripture—and for life. I want to learn how to read according to your own heart, so I can respond to you fully and freely in life. Open my mind today to your guidance and to your transforming power, and I will begin to know the true freedom of the children of God.

Contemplatio

"All time belongs to him and all the ages. To him be glory forever" (from the Easter liturgy).

Twenty-Third Sunday of Ordinary Time—
Year A

❖ ⋅ ⋅ ⋅ ⋅ ⋅ ⋅ ⋅ ⋅ ⋅ ⋅ ⋅ ⋅ ❖

Lectio

Matthew 18:15–20

Meditatio

> *"If he listens to you, you have won over your brother."*

In today's Gospel, Jesus takes up the difficult topic of giving feedback to other people, sometimes called "fraternal correction." Jesus himself did not hesitate to correct others when the occasion arose. In last Sunday's Gospel, he sharply rebuked Peter, even to the point of calling him "Satan," when Peter objected to Jesus' talk of his sufferings and death. Such correction is meant to be an act of charity for another person who may be caught up in sin or some other difficulty. Taking a person aside and gently broaching a sensitive subject is not easy. If we can't do it out of love, we shouldn't do it at all. For only a correction based on love will bear any fruit. And such love-based feedback will bear fruit when it helps the other person move away from a sin or destructive pattern of behavior.

Listening is the key here, both for the person giving the feedback and the one receiving it. To give a correction requires diplomacy and tact. A wise person will first ask the other some pertinent questions and then listen carefully, in order to understand where the person is coming from. To pull another person aside without love, to start to yell or scream, will only cause the other person to become defensive.

What if we're on the receiving end? Our pride is quick to bristle at any suggestion that we're less than perfect. But again, listening is the key. Jesus stresses, "If he listens to you. . . ." If someone else offers a criticism, a wise person will listen to it as objectively as possible. Something can be learned from it. Coaches have to give feedback to athletes so they can improve their performance. As Saint Paul reminds us, we're all in a spiritual contest with the goal of eternal life. "Run so as to win. Every athlete exercises discipline in every way" (I Cor 9:24–25). Sometimes that discipline requires us to beat back our pride and accept a rebuke.

Oratio

Jesus, help me always to speak out of charity and respect for others. If someone criticizes me, give me the humility to see what is true in their words and to learn from them. And if I need to give feedback to someone else, teach me how to do so in a way that is kind yet effective.

Contemplatio

Jesus, humble of heart, make my heart like yours.

Twenty-Third Sunday of Ordinary Time—
Year B

⋮⋯⋯⋯⋯⋯⋮

Lectio

Mark 7:31–37

Meditatio

> *"[Jesus] took him off by himself away from the crowd."*

Today's Gospel relates the healing of a man who is both deaf and mute. By healing him Jesus opens the man's ears and mouth so that he might hear and proclaim the Good News. Before that can happen, however, Jesus and the man have a private meeting. Since Jesus is traveling in Gentile territory, it is likely the man who is healed is also a Gentile. In Jesus' day it was inconceivable for a Jew to talk to, let alone touch, a non-Jew, yet Jesus does this. He goes further. Jesus draws the man away from the crowd. This isn't a case of Jesus hiding what he is about to do for fear of what his fellow Jews might think of him. Instead Jesus places all the man's needs to the forefront in order to minister to him in a personal way. If they had stayed with the crowd, the sensational healing would have been seen, but the subtly nuanced essential connection might have been missed.

What is essential here? Is it that the man is physically healed, or is it the message that God in Jesus yearns to heal the man's most profound wounds in a personal way? Hearing and proclaiming the Good News is not possible without this kind of personal encounter with the Lord. By extension we also are invited to the same. We pray with Scripture because of the way Jesus draws us apart from the crowd, from the hustle and bustle of our overloaded lives. In many Gospel accounts we read how Jesus pulls a person away from the crowd. Does that not point to the sacredness of being alone with God? Will all our problems go away, will we be immediately healed of physical infirmities because of our private moments with Jesus? Perhaps not. But the authentic encounter with God results in his grace being poured out in us, thus enabling us to hear and proclaim the Good News.

Oratio

Lord, show me how to live this intimacy with you, and give me the grace not to walk away from it. Too often I push you to the side of all my daily activities. I don't make time for you, but somehow I manage to make time for myself. The healing I seek, Lord, is not the healing of my ears and tongue, although I need those as well. I need healing on a deeper, more intimate level. Lord, take me aside—I want to go aside with you—and heal me that I might be more like you.

Contemplatio

Lord, take me aside—I want to go aside with you.

Twenty-Third Sunday of Ordinary Time— Year C

∵ · · · · · · · · · · · · ∴

Lectio

Luke 14:25–33

Meditatio

". . . be my disciple."

In today's Gospel, Saint Luke tells us that great crowds were traveling with Jesus. His teaching, demeanor, and miracles attracted them. This, however, did not make them his disciples. Jesus wants to clarify for them what it means to be his disciple. He warns that his disciples "hate" their families and even their own lives. This sounds harsh to our ears, but in Jesus' culture, overstatement was a way to get the point across. Jesus' disciples must love him more than they love their families and even their lives. They must renounce their possessions and carry their cross. His disciples must be ready to choose Jesus over anyone or anything.

It is true that we are Jesus' disciples. However, his words can challenge us to consider how committed we are to him. Following Jesus is not a matter of routine, nor is it a dry following of rules. It is not even suffering for the sake of suffering. It is loving Jesus more than we love everyone and everything else. This might seem like a tall order, almost impossible for us to fill. Yes, we love Jesus, but can we love

Jesus more than we love all else? Yes we can, with God's help . . . and God longs to do this! We learn to love Jesus gradually. The Holy Spirit accompanies us and bestows on us the graces we need for this journey in love. We only love someone whom we know . . . not just know about. It is wonderful to get to know Jesus more intimately. Simple things can help us love Jesus more: prayerful pondering of the New Testament, honest conversations with him, even just quietly being together. We grow in loving intimacy with Jesus every time we share our joys and sorrows with him, every time we make choices, even difficult ones, based on our love for him. Gradually we are transformed so that we love everyone and everything in him. Jesus has become the center of our hearts. We are truly his disciples.

Oratio

Jesus, your description of a disciple causes me to be afraid. Will I ever be able to love you more than I love anyone or anything else? I want to! I do love you! You are so lovable! But I am sometimes weak, selfish, preoccupied with unimportant things. Please help me! I want to spend quality time with you, my dearest Friend, conversing openly and confidently—speaking and listening to you. Send the Holy Spirit to transform my heart so that gradually I will love you as you deserve and love everyone and everything in you.

Contemplatio

I love you, Jesus; increase my love for you.

Monday of the Twenty-Third Week of Ordinary Time

⟡ · · · · · · · · · · · · ⟡

Lectio

Luke 6:6–11

Meditatio

> *"But they became enraged and discussed together*
> *what they might do to Jesus."*

This Gospel selection is a microcosm of Luke's message in his Gospel and Acts of the Apostles. A man with a withered hand needs healing. The Pharisees are watching Jesus closely, seeking a reason to report him to the authorities. For Luke, to be full of grace, to be favored with the gracious acts of God's kindness, requires listening, trust, and obedience.

Mary, the first to be addressed as "full of grace," is the fullest example of listening and trusting obedience. She bows before a mystery that she could not have completely comprehended, but to which she gives her whole life. Zechariah is punished for not trusting. Simeon and Anna are praised for their trusting prayers. The poor, the sick, the sinners who have nothing of their own in which to trust and who entirely depend on God's mercy are called blessed. But woe is spoken to those who are popular, praised, and wealthy, those who trust in their own ideas, self-sufficiency, and righteousness.

In these six verses of Luke we see a poor man with a withered hand simply sitting in the assembly in the synagogue. He is probably minding his own business, possibly wondering if he has the courage to ask Jesus to heal him. The Pharisees, however, have closed their minds and hearts to Jesus well before this meeting in the synagogue. They cannot hear him because his message contradicts everything they have felt to be true about how their lives should be lived. They cannot trust this dangerous young rabbi because the threat of the occupying power destroying their nation is too much for them. They cannot obey him because they have made up their minds to stop him from preaching and healing. In this passage we must face ourselves: what inspirations or invitations are we shutting out of our lives because of fear of what that change would mean? What we defend ourselves against could very well be the remedy offered to us for our salvation.

Oratio

Father, so often I've discovered that precisely what I feared the most and fought against turned out to be just what I needed. Eventually I came to my senses. Every day you speak to me and invite me to change, to move from reacting, to deeply intentional ways of living and being. Help me to hear the hard word, to trust you, and to obey.

Contemplatio

Father, I am listening.

Tuesday of the Twenty-Third Week
of Ordinary Time

⋮ ⋯⋯⋯⋯ ⋮

Lectio

Luke 6:12–19

Meditatio

" . . . he spent the night in prayer. . . ."

The image of Jesus alone on the mountain, praying through the night, has filled the consciousness of the Church from apostolic times. In imitation of Jesus, many have spent the night or some part of it in sincere and fervent prayer. What is it about prayer at night that seems so special and intense? Perhaps just the fact that this time is usually spent in a very different way—sleeping—makes keeping vigil in prayer at night seem more serious and determined.

In some communities of contemplative religious, members get up during the night for prayer. And in churches that have perpetual adoration, some people prefer the nighttime hours. When you have to make an important decision or have a special prayer need, you may find it beneficial to pray at night. Jesus' prayer before his choice of the twelve apostles is also an example for us.

But if it isn't feasible to pray in the late hours, you can find other ways to unite with Jesus in his prayer at night. Instead of reading a novel at bedtime, or falling asleep watching TV, consider taking that time for prayer instead. You can read and reflect on Scripture, pray the rosary, or simply talk to Jesus about your day. These activities may help you fall asleep more peacefully. Or, if you suffer from chronic or occasional insomnia, perhaps you can take some of the time you lie awake to pray for yourself and for others. As the psalmist prayed, "When I think of you upon my bed, through the night watches I will recall / That you indeed are my help, and in the shadow of your wings I shout for joy" (Ps 63:7–8).

Oratio

At night, so many people need prayer. Jesus, be with all those who lie awake at night in fear, grief, worry, or hunger. Be with those who work at night. Be with those who sin at night—call them back to you. Be with mothers and fathers who get up during the night to take care of their children.

Jesus, you felt the need for prolonged prayer with your Father the night before you chose your twelve apostles. Help me remember to follow your example and to pray before making decisions—big or little—so that I open myself to your guidance. At this time, I ask in particular that you help me with _____.

Contemplatio

Bless the Lord through the night.

Wednesday of the Twenty-Third Week of Ordinary Time

:⋯⋯⋯⋯:

Lectio

Luke 6:20–26

Meditatio

"Raising his eyes toward his disciples [Jesus] said. . . ."

The Beatitudes as related by Luke sound different from the more familiar ones in the Gospel of Matthew. Luke's are explicitly directed at the disciples. Matthew's seem less personal, although the context shows that there, too, the disciples are the primary audience. In Luke's list, the disciples are praised for the sacrifices they're making and are called to sacrifice even more, sharing in the sufferings of the Master. This Lucan version of the Beatitudes must be consoling to anyone who has been marginalized. People who are better off, on the other hand, may justifiably squirm when confronted with the *woes*. (It's helpful to note that the woes are warnings, not predictions or curses.)

After presenting the four woes, which are unique to his Gospel, Luke offers an antidote—the same challenge to "go beyond" that we find in Matthew's Sermon on the Mount. Jesus' followers are not to cling to the letter of the law but to live by its spirit, the twofold commandment to love God and neighbor. Both Luke and Matthew tell us that Jesus urged his followers to be impartially generous toward both the good and the bad, in imitation of the Father in heaven.

They fit together well—the Beatitudes and the twofold Great Commandment of love, lived in the freedom of God's responsible children. Since the Lord doesn't let himself be outdone in generosity, his people often begin to enjoy the reward of the Beatitudes even on this earth. I once heard of a teenager who took the motto JOY—Jesus, Others, Yourself. It seems that he picked up on this very point. Both the Beatitudes and the woes lead to a moment of decision. Are we resolved to live the Beatitudes as Jesus did, and love God and neighbor with generous hearts? If so, let's prepare for joy!

Oratio

Father, Son, and Holy Spirit, so often I find in the teachings of Jesus that you've turned everything upside down! You say joy comes from poverty, hunger, sorrow, and persecution! How can it be? Yet, I do recall times of privation when I was strangely happy. This had to be your grace, my God. Where else can such consolations have come from? Help me to learn the logic of the Gospel, which stands the world on its head.

Contemplatio

JOY—Jesus, Others, Yourself.

Thursday of the Twenty-Third Week of Ordinary Time

: · · · · · · · · · · · :

Lectio

Luke 6:27–38

Meditatio

"Do good . . . pray for . . . give . . . love . . . forgive. . . ."

When I read this section of Jesus' teachings, I always seem to snag on the part where Jesus says, "the measure with which you measure will . . . be measured out to you." It makes me shiver when I imagine the half plateful that would be placed in front of me! Jesus' words make me reflect on how generous I am to others. He is giving us a way of life based on honesty, lending, gentility, loving concern, and selfless giving. Am I up to the challenge?

I imagine that Jesus is speaking to a large group of people who *want* to hear what he is teaching, people who are more interested in the trials and challenges of everyday life than in the intricacies of the Law. Jesus is sharing his view of a life lived as God's child, and it is a picture of light, goodness, reaching out, mercy—all done with the great courage that comes from believing the best about one another. Jesus is asking *me* to live that life. This is his recipe for a life of love. The ingredients are truly demanding! Still, I cannot turn my back on his words if I want to be among the "children of the Most High."

I wonder how this lesson would sound if it were put on prime-time TV as an advertisement. How very *not* Wall Street these words of Jesus would sound. But their force and value for today's world and my life cannot be ignored. In the last decade we have seen how misplaced confidence in money, careless monitoring, and unchecked greed have carried us to the brink and damaged the trust upon which relationships in every society are built. But I know that Jesus has redeemed the world, through a relationship full of eternal, infinite love. We can always trust and learn from this infinite love.

Oratio

Jesus, I ask you to give me the courage I need to look at everyone with the eyes of love, not suspicion. If I want to follow you, I need to begin with myself and help to transform our world. I want to place my footsteps firmly in those you traced out for us all, you who are the only true Way. Trust is the big stumbling block for me, Jesus. Teach me to trust you and others. Give me some of the infinite goodness of your heart, a heart that knows the secrets and yearnings of every heart, and loves us all into gratitude and hope.

Contemplatio

Jesus, make my heart like yours.

Friday of the Twenty-Third Week of Ordinary Time

∶···········∶

Lectio

Luke 6:39–42

Meditatio

> " . . . *then you will see clearly* . . ."

I first encountered a blind person when I was eleven years old. He was an entertainer, and my brother and I were invited to meet him. When we were introduced, the blind man reached out and took my hand. To this day I wonder how he knew where my hand was.

In today's Gospel, Jesus uses images and short parables of blindness to warn his disciples, and us, against deliberate blindness of heart. The description of the two blind persons leading each other and ending up in a ditch would be funny if it wasn't so pitiful. Jesus is warning his disciples and us not to get lost in little things to the point that we fail to see God acting in our daily lives and become spiritually blind, just like the two people in the parable.

Jesus challenges the disciples to apply his teaching not only intellectually, but also with their hearts and wills. He challenges us as well. If we take time for prayer, reflective reading of the Scriptures, and a daily examination on our relationships, we discover how today's lesson applies to our lives. Jesus develops his teaching almost as if he anticipates our reasoning. How much clearer could he be with us? "Remove the wooden beam from your eye first; then you will see clearly to remove the splinter in your brother's eye." First, we need to make sure we are on the right path, or at least admit we need to change directions before trying to set someone else straight. As followers of Jesus, we are called to be Christ in the world. Our Christian faith demands that we remove whatever blocks or blurs our vision of Jesus, because each of us is to be a light in a world of darkness. All we have to do is take the plank out of our own eye so we can see Jesus clearly and follow him.

Oratio

Jesus, you challenge me to reflect on how I am living your word. Give me the courage to face those areas of my life that I am afraid to look at. I know you are with me so I won't be walking alone. Remove the blindness that hinders me from seeing your action in my life. Lord, take away the planks that block me from receiving your love and mercy. May the light of your love shine in and through me. May I see with your eyes.

Contemplatio

Jesus, I want to see you.

Saturday of the Twenty-Third Week of Ordinary Time

❖ · · · · · · · · · · · · ❖

Lectio

Luke 6:43–49

Meditatio

"Why do you call me, 'Lord, Lord,' but not do what I command?"

This question is as piercing today as it was two thousand years ago. With all our advances in science, technology, and psychology, human nature is still the same. We can still hear the truth, know what is good for us—and not do it. Jesus is questioning those who call him "Lord," acknowledging his authority and even his divinity, but still don't practice his teachings. At best, they hear the words but don't reflect on their meaning or apply it to their own life situations. At worst, they think they know better and refuse to obey. Jesus seems to be chiding them, saying, "You call on me for help when things go wrong, but you don't do what I tell you. Yet I show you how to avoid these troubles, how to be truly happy. I offer you life and you choose death instead. Do you believe I am Lord or not?" Jesus warns them that they are like a person who built a house without a foundation, and the floods came and totally destroyed it.

The person who listens to the Word of God and acts on it, instead, is like a person who digs a foundation and builds a house on rock. It can withstand the floodwaters. Many temptations and storms will arise in our lives. Jesus is asking us to listen to his words and take them to heart, to meditate and pray over them, to make them our own and live them out. He is the Eternal Word of the Father. He wants to live in us. Opening ourselves to his word can make this happen. God is love, and when we open ourselves to him he pours his love into our hearts. Then we in turn can share his love with others; we can love with his heart. Jesus tells us, "Whoever loves me will keep my word, and my Father will love him, and we will come to him and make our dwelling with him" (Jn 14:23).

Oratio

Dear Lord, I thank you for the great gift of your holy Scriptures. Give me the grace to keep your word in my heart, to meditate on it and to live it in my daily life. Live and act in me. Don't let me place any obstacles in your way. Strengthen me against temptation, against my weakness and fear. I know that with you I have strength for everything. I place all my trust in you.

Contemplatio

"I love you, LORD, my strength, LORD, my rock, my fortress, my deliverer" (Ps. 18:2–3).

Twenty-Fourth Sunday of Ordinary Time— Year A

∴⋯⋯⋯∴

Lectio

Matthew 18:21–35

Meditatio

> *"Should you not have had pity on your fellow servant,*
> *as I had pity on you?"*

Jesus always gives the best examples. Sometimes they seem a bit extreme, but the situations are real enough. Our own situations include credit-card debt, college loans, mortgages, medical bills, accidents, lawsuits—the list is imposing. It is easy to lose everything like the debtor in this story, and bankruptcy does affect the whole family. Fortunately, in our day a family will not be hauled off to prison. This particular story would be startlingly beautiful if it ended just as the master absolved the man's entire debt. But then the man we so pitied goes out, freed of his own burden, and viciously falls upon another man who owes him a fraction of what he himself owed. He seizes the man, chokes him, demands repayment— such violence! He has learned nothing from the mercy shown him. The second man collapses to his knees, begging for patience. Nothing doing. He gets no more time, no mercy. The man who had been forgiven moments before now demands full restitution.

Strangely, the characters in this story expect repayment from those thrown into prison. It appears that this is not a case of money required, but of revenge. Wouldn't it be better to forgive a debt that can't reasonably be repaid? The last injustice here is worse than the first. As a result, third parties who know both men report to the merciful master what has happened. The Gospel says that he was incensed by the insensitivity of the man he had forgiven. He has him apprehended and hands him over to the torturer until he can pay back the last penny. We realize that this is just a story that Jesus told. However, the lesson is real even today. We cannot expect the Lord's mercy for our transgressions unless we forgive others from the heart.

Oratio

Dear Lord, why is it so easy to demand our due from others? Sometimes coming out of the confessional after begging forgiveness for our sins, we find ourselves harassing a family member or a friend. We demand that they give us what is ours. It may be a small matter like an offense against good manners or an imagined insult, or it could be a more serious situation. In any case, help me to treat others with the mercy you have shown me. Lord, keep your words alive in my heart, "Forgive us our trespasses as we forgive those who trespass against us." Amen.

Contemplatio

Be merciful as I am with you.

Twenty-Fourth Sunday of Ordinary Time—
Year B

⁘ · · · · · · · · · · · · ⁘

Lectio

Mark 8:27–35

Meditatio

"You are thinking not as God does. . . ."

The disciples have been following Jesus for a good while. They have seen him in action and have heard his words spoken with authority. Most important, they have seen that he lives what he preaches. Now Jesus wants to know what they are thinking in his regard. Do they believe in him? Have they understood who he really is and why he has come into their lives and into the world? At first it seems that Peter "gets it." He confidently exclaims, "You are the Christ." But Peter's vision of the Messiah does not coincide with that of Jesus. Jesus describes what he must undergo, saying that he "must suffer greatly and be rejected by the elders, the chief priests, and the scribes, and be killed, and rise after three days." This overwhelms Peter and clashes with his ideas, so he adamantly rejects it. It cannot be this way.

While he understands Peter's human way of thinking, Jesus must be faithful to his mission and wants to lead Peter beyond his narrow human perspective. Jesus is always inviting us "beyond." He loves and accepts us where we are, but he wants to move us beyond, into a way of thinking, feeling, and living that is in tune with his own. In this, Jesus' constant reference point is the Father. The goal of Jesus' life is to be faithful to the Father's plan of love for humanity. Like Peter, we can easily get stuck in our narrow, human perspective. Without the teachings, example, and grace of Jesus, we remain stuck. But in every situation, Jesus is at our side, inviting us to see things just a little bit differently, to think about reality with a God-perspective that can change our lives. Is there a situation in my life right now that God is inviting me to see in a different way?

Oratio

Jesus, my Lord, how my mind needs conversion! Yes, I have a tendency to think that my way of seeing things, my judgments, and my perspectives are the best. But today you invite me to move beyond all that. You invite me to open my mind to new possibilities and perspectives that flow from the mind of the Father, who is Truth and Love. Give me the courage I need to let go of my ways of thinking and open myself to your plan and your way of self-giving love.

Contemplatio

Make your own the mind of Christ Jesus (see Phil 2:5).

Twenty-Fourth Sunday of Ordinary Time— Year C

∴ · · · · · · · · · · · · ∴

Lectio

Luke 15:1–32

Meditatio

> *"Rejoice with me because I have found my lost sheep."*

Today's liturgy sets before us three parables that center on God's mercy and love. This love is an incredible, almost ridiculous love that knows no bounds, welcoming all in its embrace. Jesus tells the story of the Good Shepherd. A group of tax collectors and sinners gathers eagerly around Jesus, hanging on his every word. With his keen eye, Jesus does not direct his parable to this interested, attentive group. Instead he speaks to a group of self-righteous bystanders. Some Pharisees are standing on the side, complaining that "This man welcomes sinners and eats with them." Doesn't he know who these people are? Perhaps by directing his message to them—and to us—Jesus wants to show how outrageous is his love, a love that welcomes sinners in its embrace.

"What man among you having a hundred sheep and losing one of them," he asks them, "would not leave the ninety-nine in the desert and go after the lost one until he finds it?" This is crazy, utterly ridiculous! No sane person would leave ninety-nine strong, healthy sheep at risk in the desert in order to rescue one who is weak and fragile. Who would do such a thing? No one who has any sense. Would I? Would I risk all I have to save the small, insignificant, fragile one? Yet this is precisely the point. Jesus' love does not make sense. It is a crazy, passionate, utterly ridiculous love. It is a love that risks all it has to save the one. It is a love that embraces everyone, even the sinner who stands condemned and alone. It is a love that embraces the undesirables, the persons whom I look down upon, those who in my judgment count for nothing. Am I ready to love in this way? Am I prepared to love to this extent?

Oratio

Jesus, your love is a crazy love, one that is utterly ridiculous in the eyes of the world. It is a love that risks all in order to gain the one. Teach me to love in this way. Teach me to widen my horizons so my love can be crazy and ridiculous, like yours.

Contemplatio

Jesus, live and love in me!

Monday of the Twenty-Fourth Week of Ordinary Time

∴⋯⋯⋯∴

Lectio

Luke 7:1–10

Meditatio

> " . . . I am not worthy to have you enter under my roof . . .
> but say the word. . . ."

The centurion in today's Gospel is an interesting character. He is part of the Roman occupying force, but he built the local synagogue. The Jewish elders respect him. A cynic might say the centurion was merely good at small-town politics, but then we see that he even cares about a dying slave in his household. This centurion is on the road of responding to God's invitation. Yet he is more than just an enigmatic figure in the Gospel narrative, for we repeat his words at every celebration of Mass: *I am not worthy . . . but say the word. . . .*

Grace—God's life active in this world and in our lives—is a gift. God always has the first move. He created us in his image and likeness. With no prior merit or action on our part (we didn't even exist) we are born into this world, already in the image of the Son. For those of us who were baptized as infants, this truth is carried even further. We were brought into God's family, the Church, through no effort or merit on our part. It is all a gift—pure gift. The first question is, will I open up the gift, treasure it, and put it to good use? Well, obviously that has happened to some extent or I wouldn't be here actively reflecting on the Liturgy of the Word for today. So then the question for me is not so much will I respond to God's first move; I've made a second move. The real question is: who gets the third move? Has my response to God's gracious invitation taken on a life of its own to the point where God has a minor role to play in the whole enterprise? Or do I bear in mind that there is no question of earning God's favor or being worthy of his grace?

Oratio

Yes, I am actively engaged in an exchange of gift and response with you, Lord. You have literally given your life for me, and you continue to pour your life of grace into my heart. I am given to you in Baptism and I want to continue giving my life to you in my daily words and actions. But I am overwhelmed at your generosity in entering into such an uneven relationship, Lord. You are God—and I am only your creature. I am not worthy of you, but your word heals this rift between us.

Contemplatio

God *always* has the first move.

Tuesday of the Twenty-Fourth Week of Ordinary Time

⁘ ⋯⋯⋯⋯ ⁘

Lectio

Luke 7:11–17

Meditatio

> *"Jesus gave him to his mother."*

As is customary, the men of the village lead the way, followed by the stretcher bearing the body—the body of her son. She shuffles along behind the bier, head down and tears dripping into the dust of the road. Behind her walk the other women of Nain. The music of flutes and the wailing of professional mourners fills the air. It had all happened so suddenly. Of necessity the body has to be buried on the same day her son died. She can't wrap her mind around it: the form on the stretcher, with the white cloth over his face, is her own dear boy, the only survivor of his siblings. He is also her sole support—her provider and protector. Or rather, he *had been* all this. The full import of what is happening washes over her, and she almost stumbles.

She realizes that someone is walking beside her. "Don't cry," says a deep voice. She looks up, blinks back the tears, and meets the compassionate gaze of—who? The man touches the stretcher, and the bearers stop. Then the unbelievable happens. He tells her son to get up; the young man sits up straight. Someone removes the cloth from his face, and he begins to ask: "What's happening? What am I doing on this . . . ?" Meanwhile, the itinerant rabbi takes the mother by the arm and brings her to her son.

Thinking about this, I realize that something hasn't changed since that time. First-century Israel had its marginalized people, which included widows and orphans. Twenty-first century North America has its own marginalized people—a list too lengthy to enumerate. We might have opportunities to help some of these fellow human beings materially, but there's something else we can always do. We can remember them in prayer.

Oratio

God, my Father, today I ask you to especially bless these people whom I do not know but *you* know: the marginalized teenager in the nearest high school; the new immigrant family in town; the lonely widower in the most poorly run nursing home in our area; the neglected child in our school system; the needy, unwed mother in this county. Grant to these persons the grace and courage they need to deal with their situations. Inspire men and women to reach out to them in Christian compassion, bringing each of them the possibility of a brighter future. I ask this in Jesus' name. Amen.

Contemplatio

O God, visit your people again!

Wednesday of the Twenty-Fourth Week of Ordinary Time

∴ · · · · · · · · · · · · ∴

Lectio

Luke 7:31–35

Meditatio

> " . . . wisdom . . . vindicated. . . ."

Like bookends, the Gospel texts this week surround the cynicism of Jesus' opponents in today's reading with the earlier openness of the centurion and the mourners of Nain, along with that of tomorrow's penitent woman. Jesus is challenged to validate himself and his mission on his detractors' terms. He refuses. Their ambivalence is nothing more than a smokescreen for their fear of commitment and unwillingness to change. They'll straddle the fence indefinitely rather than risk being proved wrong about Jesus.

During the U.S. Civil War, Confederate General Joseph Johnston was an eminent strategist and a courageous soldier. But he was also stymied by his demand for perfection. In critical moments, his fear of failure paralyzed him from attacking. By singling out one consideration or another as sufficient reason for not moving, he avoided defeat . . . and blame. Actually, his dallying resulted in a string of missed opportunities, which ultimately contributed to the fall of the Confederacy.

Artful dodgers that they are, Christ's critics adopt a similar strategy. Demand perfection and you can sidestep a commitment to discipleship. Fix the imperative to change on someone or something else, and presto!—personal responsibility vanishes. But whose standards determine what is "perfect"? When people refuse to acknowledge "the righteousness of God," Luke says, they reject "the plan of God for themselves" (7:30). They don't believe the formula for personal reform is evangelically simple: grace plus the decision to change (made over and over). They will not be led, then laughed at when they "fail." Jesus says, "But wisdom is vindicated by all her children." Those who do something with their lives do make mistakes, but those who do nothing make the greatest mistake of all. Nothing, not even death on a cross, is beyond the pale of redemption.

Oratio

Jesus, do you understand how afraid I am to change? To be vulnerable? To fail? I would rather justify my attitudes and actions than lose my certitude. It's my rudder, my north star—and it's attached to the experiences of my life. Take me, fear and all. Once more, I resolve to tell myself each day that I can change, whether I believe it at first or not. You know it, and that's enough for me.

Contemplatio

Lord, strengthen my inconstant resolve with your unfailing grace.

Thursday of the Twenty-Fourth Week of Ordinary Time

:·············:

Lectio

Luke 7:36–50

Meditatio

"Do you see this woman?"

Simon the Pharisee bears a striking resemblance to another man in Luke's Gospel: the Pharisee in the parable who found himself in the Temple with a tax collector. Like the unnamed Pharisee, Simon assumes he knows the other person's relationship with God. Jesus, as usual, responds to the occasion with a parable, this time about two debtors. If the woman, because she is forgiven much, shows great love, Simon needs forgiveness for his "lesser" debt, too.

Simon may not have had any big-ticket items on his debit sheet with God, but as Jesus lists his *omissions*, one by one, it all seems to add up to a kind of contempt—or at the very least, indifference toward Jesus. Even the fact of the lesser debt is a sign of equal, if not greater, weakness on his part: it is one thing to be incapable of repaying an enormous sum—but to need to have a paltry debt written off? Simon just doesn't have eyes to see how much God in his mercy has forgiven him. He can't take his eyes off the woman at Jesus' feet.

Neither can Jesus. At the end of his life, when Jesus himself wants to make a striking statement about the reverence, love, and humility his disciples owe one another, he will do for his disciples something very much like what this woman did for him. He knows the image will stay with the disciples.

Oratio

Jesus, why did Simon even invite you to dinner? You came to his house, but he did not say, "Lord, I am not worthy that you should enter" (see Lk 7:6). Maybe he was so busy monitoring his fulfillment of all the precepts of the Law that he didn't have any interior space left to attend to you, much less become aware of what was still lacking. Omissions aren't addressed because we notice them; they come about because our attention is misdirected! Help me keep my gaze on you, and to begin to see as you see: not omissions as such, but the glory of God in all things.

Contemplatio

"I keep the LORD ever before me" (Ps 16:8).

Friday of the Twenty-Fourth Week of Ordinary Time

⁝············⁝

Lectio

Luke 8:1–3

Meditatio

> *"accompanying . . . provided for them. . . ."*

This Gospel passage about the Galilean women follows the story of the sinful woman who loves much because much has been forgiven her. We are told that because of her deep love for Jesus she anoints his feet; she has accepted God's forgiveness and her heart overflows in response. In a way that story of responding to God's love, forgiveness, and healing continues here.

These women accompany and provide for Jesus and the disciples in response to the invitation to love. All these women have a story—we know, for example, that Mary Magdalene was freed from seven demons. They have each experienced firsthand God's love, forgiveness, and healing in such an overwhelming way that their hearts are flooded with a desire to love in response.

In *Adeste*, a Christmas song written by our sisters, a line says, "what can I give him, the Lord of creation?" The response is, "hearts that are eager to love without measure, to

Bethlehem's poor child are presents of gold." We too are faced with the question of how to respond to God's love.

Luke's Gospel is vague on exactly what these women provided—and what a gift this vagueness is. It doesn't so much matter how what they did, as *that* they did it. As in the song, God is asking us to respond to his love by loving through thoughts, words, and actions. The women in today's Gospel answer the call to love by accompanying and providing for Jesus and the disciples. Each of us lives this love and service in different ways, whether we are married, single, or in the consecrated life. Yet we all do this in response to and as witnesses of God's love in our lives.

Oratio

Jesus, each day you flood me with your love and innumerable blessings. You have carried me when I have been at my lowest points and danced with me when I have rejoiced. My heart overflows with the love with which you have filled it. May I this day allow this love, the love you have given me, to flow over to others that they, too, may find you and praise you. Give me the grace to serve my brothers and sisters as you invite me to love them unreservedly, just as you love me. Amen.

Contemplatio

Jesus Life, may my presence bring grace and consolation everywhere!

Saturday of the Twenty-Fourth Week of Ordinary Time

⁝· · · · · · · · · · · · ·⁝

Lectio

Luke 8:4–15

Meditatio

" . . . bear fruit through perseverance. . . ."

Today's parable is unusual because Jesus explains it himself. That isn't the case with most of the parables. He says the seed is the word of God. Our hearts are the seedbed where that word is sown. Will it grow and bear fruit in our lives? That's the key question.

Jesus warns us about three obstacles the seed has to overcome. One is an external obstacle: the devil. Perhaps we don't think about the devil very much nowadays, but the evil spirit is just as real as ever. Jesus says the devil tries to snatch the word of God out of hearts, lest we believe and be saved. The lesson for us is to keep careful watch, pray to the Holy Spirit, and never let evil influences into our heart.

The second obstacle is lack of nourishment. The seed withered for lack of water. Prayer is the fertilizer that will make the word of God grow in our hearts. Without prayer, the seed of God's word will die out just as surely as a plant without water will shrivel up and blow away.

Finally, Jesus tells us that the last obstacle is whatever chokes off God's word by distracting us from it. Riches and pleasures can do that, but so can anxieties. It's like walking into a room so full of clutter that it's impossible to focus on what's really important. Does that yellowed newspaper from twenty years ago make me forget about the utility bill I need to pay now? All the clutter in our hearts will choke off God's life of grace within us. We need to let go of it. Get out the spiritual trash bags and start collecting. Are old resentments still lingering? Are there old wrongs that need to be made right? When we let go of these things we will be free, and then the word of God can take root and flourish in our hearts.

Oratio

Jesus, help me to keep watch and pray so I won't be led astray by temptations but will bear abundant fruit for the kingdom. I want to let go of all the inner clutter that distracts me from you. Help me to give over to you any resentments, lack of forgiveness, or bad feelings I may have toward anyone. Make me open to your love.

Contemplatio

Lord, plant your word in my heart.

Twenty-Fifth Sunday of Ordinary Time—
Year A

⁘ · · · · · · · · · · · · ⁘

Lectio

Matthew 20:1–16

Meditatio

" . . . the last will be first, and the first will be last."

This parable strikes at the heart of a deeply held human reverence for fairness. We learn this early in childhood and seem to organize our entire lives around it. This parable brings to mind the phrase, "It's not fair!" How often we have all said that! After all, how fair is it that an employer pays those who work for nine hours the same amount as those who work for one? It isn't fair! But isn't life unfair? Perhaps what we revere as a value really isn't a value, but a way that we defend ourselves against the unfairness we face all throughout our lives.

Fairness is so deeply rooted in us that we also expect God to be fair. Thus, we hold God to our limited understanding of fairness. I have become aware that whenever we apply labels, like fairness in this case, we somehow seem justified to judge. Hidden under the guise of fairness lurks the sin of judging. For in order to gauge the fairness of a situation, we sit in judgment over others, including God.

This parable highlights for me that when we judge in this way, we expect things to be fair for only one person: ourselves. But to judge the fairness of the situation accurately, we would need to know everything and take everyone else into account, including the person we believe is being unfair.

A tremendous burden can be lifted from us if we stop using fairness as the paradigm by which we judge others, God, and situations. We can only do this if we suspend judgment, admit how little we know, and trust in the omniscience of the "landowner"—God.

Oratio

Father, your Son has told us this story about you. I have to admit that it doesn't make sense to me. If I had been one of the workers that you hired that day, I would have been angry at the unfairness of your decision to give everyone the same pay. I realize that because you know everything you, and you alone, have the capacity of judging what is truly "fair" for everyone. Help me to overcome my tendency to judge so that I can be freed from this burden that closes me in on myself. Free me. Open me to others, to you, to love. Amen.

Contemplatio

Father, may I be generous as you are generous.

Twenty-Fifth Sunday of Ordinary Time—
Year B

⁝ · · · · · · · · · · · · ⁝

Lectio

Mark 9:30–37

Meditatio

> *"If anyone wishes to be first,*
> *he shall be the last of all and the servant of all."*

This beloved Gospel scene of Jesus welcoming and embracing a child has been portrayed in stained glass and art for centuries. It is so popular that we may miss its powerful message that forever changed our understanding of service. Just before this scene, Jesus tells the apostles for a second time that he will suffer, die, and rise. Shortly after, the group begins discussing which of them is the greatest. The apostles are clearly not immune to competition!

The Gospel writer tells us that Jesus then sits down and calls the Twelve together. The Master uses this incident as an occasion to teach them. The detail that Jesus sits down is important. To teach from a sitting position symbolizes that Jesus is speaking from his authority as Teacher and Lord. Each year we are reminded of this in our liturgy when we celebrate the Chair of Saint Peter, the "chair" that symbolizes the teaching authority of the apostle whom Jesus chose to serve as the visible head of the Church.

In Jesus' time, children, women, and servants had no legal status or rights; they were considered unimportant. A free man would consider it unbecoming to serve or to do the duties of a servant or a woman. Jesus turns the standard of greatness and service upside down. His disciples are called to serve the poor and all those who cannot repay. Jesus' action of placing a child in the apostles' midst and embracing the little one is the answer to their question about greatness. To receive and to serve those who are weak, defenseless, and without worldly status is to show respect for each person's human dignity, and to receive Jesus and the Father. Jesus revealed his greatness in his humble acceptance of his passion and death and his service to all. For a disciple of Jesus, greatness lies not in domination but in openhearted service.

Oratio

Jesus, you are our Teacher and Lord. By the witness of your life and your love for the poor, the weak, and the forgotten, you teach us the dignity of every human person. Help me to receive as you would the child, the immigrant, and those who are vulnerable in any way. Take from my heart all desire for recognition, importance, and domination. May I receive the wisdom you wish to give me through the poor, and may I experience the joy that comes from loving with an open heart.

Contemplatio

Jesus, you came to serve, not to be served.

Twenty-Fifth Sunday of Ordinary Time— Year C

❖· · · · · · · · · · · ·❖

Lectio

Luke 16:1–13

Meditatio

> *"For the children of this world are more prudent in dealing with their own generation than are the children of light."*

Setting aside the confusing discussion of what the steward actually did before and after getting fired, let's look at why Jesus is telling this parable in the first place. The moral is basically that the children of light (that's us) can learn from the creative problem-solving of the steward, who represents the "children of this world." Jesus is holding up not the steward's concrete actions for us to learn from, but the prudence he shows.

In current usage, the term "prudence" is mostly associated with cautiousness, but that is not the true meaning of the word. Prudence is the virtue that helps us make sound judgments, a kind of practical wisdom. It's called a cardinal virtue (remember those?) because it is a hinge for other virtues. ("Cardinal" comes from *cardo*, the Latin word for hinge.) With prudence we can judge whether a certain action is virtuous or not. We can judge that it would be right to help someone in a particular way, or to resist some wrong being done. Then other virtues come into play in actually carrying out what we have judged to be the right thing to do—generosity in helping someone, courage to speak up about the wrong, and so forth.

Jesus looks at the steward as someone who makes a practical decision about what he should do, and then carries out the decision with energy and creativity. How much more should the children of light follow his example!

Oratio

I need to look at how prudent I am, Jesus. My goal is ultimately to spend eternity with you and to help as many people as I can to do the same. But when I look at some of my daily choices, they don't seem to be bringing me toward that goal. I sometimes live as if this life were all there is. That's not prudent. I remember times in the past when I acted with much more creativity and determination toward my goal. Jesus, help me to recover some of that zeal and energy and to live as a child of the light.

Contemplatio

I want to live as a child of light (see Eph 5:8).

Monday of the Twenty-Fifth Week of Ordinary Time

∴∙∙∙∙∙∙∙∙∙∙∙∴

Lectio

Luke 8:16–18

Meditatio

" . . . places it on a lampstand so that those who enter may see the light."

As I read this parable of Jesus, I imagine a darkened room being flooded with light when someone turns on a lamp. The light reaches to the corners of the room, illuminates faces and surfaces, and transforms a dark place into a warmly lit home. In this parable and those preceding it, Jesus is speaking of his word, which is a gift for us to embrace with generous and faithful hearts. The word has power to enlighten and to make us vessels of that indescribable light. Jesus has gifted his word with the power and the qualities of light: power that makes light streak across the universe at an unbelievable speed, qualities that unfold in the spectacle of the northern lights and shimmer in the most delicate rainbow.

Jesus' word has its own divine power. Jesus could have arranged for his preaching to be imprinted directly on the minds of all humans without any intermediary. But Jesus is all about relationships—his with each of us, and ours with one another. His word is given to build and strengthen relationships, as it reveals the Father's love and plan. Jesus wants us to spread his word, to be the light, to join him in that slow, loving process of revelation that eventually will make all things visible and bring all secrets to light.

Even the revelation of the secrets of the natural world produces wonder. I think, for example, of the look of illumination on Helen Keller's young face when, helped by Anne Sullivan, she understood the concept of water. Or I recall the amazement on the faces of people who contemplate works of art or creativity. Yet how much greater are the mysteries of faith that Jesus gives us in the Gospel. I want to help others experience the wonder and happiness of faith by sharing the Lord's word. I only need to be a willing transmitter of the Lord's light and to stay out of God's way as he shines through me.

Oratio

Lord Jesus, help me to keep my gaze on you and not get lost along the way. But how often I need to call for your help, because I have lost the thread of your message! As I move through this life, I beg you for the light that I know you want to pour into my heart and soul. I beg it for myself, but also for all those you have placed along my path, with whom I am to share the light's brilliance. Help me to remember that, no matter how dark all might seem around me, your light dwells within, and I, like you, will share it through love.

Contemplatio

Lord, be my light!

Tuesday of the Twenty-Fifth Week of Ordinary Time

∴∙∙∙∙∙∙∙∙∙∙∙∙∙∴

Lectio

Luke 8:19–21

Meditatio

> *"My mother and my brothers are those*
> *who hear the word of God and act on it."*

At first glance, we may find these words of Jesus baffling. Does he really mean that those who act on God's word are closer to him than his own blood relations? Pondering this raises the question: what is the word of God and what does it mean to act on it? Jesus was sent by the Father to redeem humanity from sin and to teach the way of salvation. Jesus redeemed us once and for all, but each of us is free to accept salvation and order our lives according to it. We have a choice. Jesus saved us, but we have to want that salvation and to live as people who are redeemed. We can do that by following Jesus' teachings. His teachings are not rules imposed upon us to make life difficult, but are invitations to find happiness. The human person's most basic desire is for happiness, and Jesus' commandments lead us on the way to find it.

An example of this can be found in the movie *The Blind Side*. It depicts the selfless sacrifice of the Tuohy family. This well-to-do white family welcome into their home Michael Oher, a homeless African American youth. In the process the family finds a joy that only following Jesus' teaching to "love one's neighbor" can give. We are made for the good and noble life. When we cheat, steal, insult, lie, and hate, we hurt ourselves as well as others, and we drift farther away from our deepest desire—happiness. But when we act on the word of God, we make the words of Jesus a reality in our day-to-day lives. We try to be gentle, patient, generous, forgiving, merciful, and trusting. When we act in this way, we grow close to the Master who longs for our love. Let us ask our Lord to give us the grace to examine in our hearts how we put the word into practice in our lives. Only then will we become authentic members of Jesus' family of disciples.

Oratio

Jesus, Word of Life, make your word take root in my heart today so that I may reflect your joy to the world. Your mother listened most closely to your word and lived it out. May her life give encouragement to all your disciples, and an example of finding happiness in you.

Contemplatio

"Your word is a lamp for my feet, a light for my path" (Ps 119:105).

Wednesday of the Twenty-Fifth Week of Ordinary Time

:·············:

Lectio

Luke 9:1–6

Meditatio

"He sent them to proclaim the Kingdom of God and to heal the sick."

In today's Gospel the apostles go out on mission to proclaim the Good News, heal the sick, and cast out demons. Jesus gives them the power and the authority to do it. God's word is efficacious—whatever God says, happens. When God says, "Let there be light," there is light (Gn 1:3). When Jesus sends the Twelve to proclaim the kingdom, it spreads. When they speak words of healing, the blind see, the deaf hear, and the lame walk. The apostles' unshakable faith is so great it can't be contained. Today's Gospel tells us they "went from village to village proclaiming the good news and curing diseases everywhere." *Everywhere!* They can't keep the Good News to themselves. They have to tell everyone about it— those who would accept it and those who would reject it. Jesus' injunction to shake the dust from their feet if they are not welcome encourages them to keep going and not let hardships or opposition stop them or slow them down.

He sends them out without food, money, or even a second tunic to keep them warm. On another occasion he spoke of how his heavenly Father feeds the birds and clothes the flowers. Now Jesus asks his disciples to be a sign and witness to the loving, providential care of God. They are to trust completely in his promise, "Seek first the kingdom of God and his righteousness, and all these things will be given you besides" (Mt 6:33). Jesus realizes the kingdom in their lives and in the lives of those with whom they share the word, those they heal—the kingdom of truth, goodness, and love, where God is all in all, where all live as children of the same heavenly Father. The Good News is the same for us today. God's word is alive! The kingdom is in our midst. We need only to open our minds and our hearts and trust completely in God so that the transforming power of the Gospel may change us and the world.

Oratio

Lord, your word is as living and effective today as when you first spoke it on earth. Give me the faith and trust of the apostles, so that I may proclaim your message joyfully and faithfully to all those whose lives I touch, so that I may do what you want to do through me. Let me seek you and your kingdom above all else, and trust that you will take care of me. Let me bring your light and love to this poor, broken world. Live in me, O Lord.

Contemplatio

"Your Kingdom come, your will be done" (Mt 6:10).

Thursday of the Twenty-Fifth Week of Ordinary Time

∴ · · · · · · · · · · · · ∴

Lectio

Luke 9:7–9

Meditatio

"Who then is this about whom I hear such things?"

Herod wants to see Jesus. But why? Luke tells us that during Jesus' passion, Herod was eager to see him because he hoped to witness a miracle. But at this point in the Gospel, that doesn't seem to be the case. Herod muses, "John I beheaded. Who then is this . . . ?" Possible translation: "Has John returned?" I think Herod's past is coming back to haunt him. He had been fascinated by the Baptist, entranced by that eloquent, persuasive personality. He hadn't wanted John killed. Herodias, his consort, had desired and achieved it. But, of course, he, Herod, had been an instrument. Perhaps the tetrarch is now struggling with remorse. I can imagine him, restless by night and fretful by day—half hopeful, half fearful that the Baptist had returned.

Of course, Herod wasn't the only historical person to be haunted by his past. Many have been. Perhaps that's why storytellers and writers often tell about real people or fictitious characters dogged by memories of their former deeds—like Shakespeare's Lady Macbeth.

And what about myself? Is something haunting me? If so, facing and analyzing it might enable me to put it in its place and move on. Otherwise, a spiritual director or counselor might be able to help me sort things out.

It isn't helpful to continually recall the past with a sense of guilt or, for that matter, to look toward the future with anxiety. God lives in eternity, which is an "everlasting now." The place for us to get in touch with him is our own "now." That's where we can find God's grace and joy. That's where we can serve him and others, as well as store up a lasting treasure in heaven (see Lk 12:33). "Now" is our Father's great gift to us—his present.

Oratio

My God and Father, I thank you for my past, with all its ups and downs. But I want to acknowledge it and move on. I thank you for the future, too, whatever it may be. But I don't want to lose the precious "now" while worrying about my future. Help me to recognize the treasure you have given me: the sacrament of the present moment. If lived well, the present is where I encounter your Son and the grace of the Holy Spirit. It's been called a wellspring of holiness. Thank you for this gift, Father. I want to cherish it and use it well.

Contemplatio

". . . now is a very acceptable time . . . now is the day of salvation" (2 Cor 6:2).

Friday of the Twenty-Fifth Week of Ordinary Time

:·············:

Lectio

Luke 9:18–22

Meditatio

"He rebuked them. . . ."

Jesus sharply forbids the apostles to reveal who he is. That doesn't make sense! God had come on the earth in the person of Jesus to reconcile us to himself. Surely a well-planned announcement that Jesus is the Messiah would be in order. Why not tell everyone? But no, Jesus forbids any mention of it. Instead he talks about suffering, dying, and rising on the third day. This passage comes shortly before Luke's account of the Transfiguration. Jesus brings the three apostles closest to him up on the mountaintop, and they see Jesus in his glory. "Let's stay here!" Peter cries out in awe. Many months later he will flee from Mount Calvary. He had not listened to Jesus' words: "The Son of Man must suffer greatly and be rejected by the elders, the chief priests, and the scribes, and be killed and on the third day be raised."

Our lives too swing between these two mounts—the mount of consolation and joy, and the mount of suffering and shame. Like Peter, we may find ourselves eager to declare our faith in Christ as the Son of God. We may find it easy to believe when everything in life is going our way. However, when Calvary edges into our life with its darkness and confusion, we can easily forget the words of today's Gospel: *I and you will suffer greatly*. We forget that the Mount of the Transfiguration and the Mount of Calvary are simply two sides of the glory Jesus came to reveal. We let our plans, egos, and anxiety take over, and we refuse to hear the promise of darkness and suffering as followers of Jesus' way. No one wants to hear these difficult words of Jesus. But to proclaim them is a gift to others, for whether we like it or not, despite all our plans, shadows and sunlight dance across everyone's days. These words of Jesus give us meaning and purpose, and comfort us when dark days come.

Oratio

I adore you, my Lord, as the Suffering Servant, as the Good Shepherd who lays down his life, as our Savior risen from death and living forevermore!

Contemplatio

In joy and in sorrow, you are with me, my Lord.

Saturday of the Twenty-Fifth Week
of Ordinary Time

:•·············•:

Lectio

Luke 9:43b–45

Meditatio

". . . they were afraid to ask him. . . ."

Fear. It is one of the most-mentioned emotions in the Bible. Fear can be good when it prevents us from doing something foolish like stepping into a busy street without checking for oncoming cars. More often than not, however, fear is simply debilitating. Fear can grip us and prevent us from doing what's best for us, from doing what God wants us to do. That is why so often throughout the Bible, God tells his people not to be afraid.

Today's Gospel relates in a few verses the second time Jesus tells his apostles about his upcoming passion, death, and resurrection. They are just as confused as ever about what it all means. Instead of voicing their concerns, they give in to fear. They keep their questions to themselves and, in a way, prevent Jesus from explaining further and giving them comfort. Where does this fear come from? Has Jesus proven himself to be so unapproachable that his closest followers are afraid to ask him a question? Of course not. Jesus has time and again proven that he cares about them and would answer their questions. It seems almost ludicrous that any person then or today would be afraid to talk to Jesus, to God. But fear is not always a logical emotion.

We, too, experience this fear. Perhaps we feel out of control, isolated, or overwhelmed. Regardless of the situation, we can turn to Jesus in prayer for answers, comfort, and hope. He is waiting for us to go to him, to run to him, and to place before him our cares and concerns. Even if the problems and situations don't disappear, we know he is with us, giving us the grace we need to handle them.

Oratio

Of all the things in life that I could fear, you, Lord, are not among them. You love me in a way that sometimes boggles my mind. I know that I can approach you about everything, but sometimes I find myself trying to handle things on my own. Yet you invite me to share everything with you. I don't want to hold anything back from you, Jesus. Today, I bring you my joys and tears, my hopes and concerns; give me the grace, Lord, to bring my entire self to you.

Contemplatio

Be not afraid; I am with you.

Twenty-Sixth Sunday of Ordinary Time— Year A

∴ · · · · · · · · · · · · · ∴

Lectio

Matthew 21:28–32

Meditatio

> " . . . *change your minds and believe*. . . ."

I've always been amazed at the incredible teamwork of acrobats. They have to have a blind trust in their teammates. They have to believe that when they let go of the bar and reach out, someone else will grasp their hands. The timing and the gracefulness make it so thrilling and beautiful.

Letting go is a theme in today's Gospel. Two sons are having trouble letting go of their own plans so as to take hold of their father's. The parable involves making a choice and changing one's mind. Unlike trained acrobats, these two sons swing back and forth, unsure of whether they want to let go and do their father's will. The father calls his sons to work in the vineyard, inviting them to let go of selfishness and to use their gifts for others.

Throughout the day God constantly communicates with us in different ways. He is calling us into the vineyard too. God allows us to be in certain situations, with certain people, so we may use our gifts to love and serve others. God knows how we can serve others at the right time and moves us to "show up" there, just as one acrobat is at the right place at the right time to catch the other.

· We can learn from the parable of the two sons that it's never too late to change our minds. At times it's hard to let go of the bar, figuratively speaking, and trust that someone will catch us in the air. God reaches out to grasp our hands when we let go of our plans and surrender to his. What beautiful things can happen then.

Oratio

Jesus, you are the faithful Son who heard the Father's call to work in the vineyard and immediately did your Father's will. Help me to let go of all that I grasp so tightly, which keeps me from entering the vineyard of my heavenly Father. When I choose my own will, give me the grace to change my mind and experience the miracles that happen when I put my hands in yours.

Contemplatio

I will go into the vineyard.

Twenty-Sixth Sunday of Ordinary Time—Year B

∴ · · · · · · · · · · · · ∴

Lectio

Mark 9:38–43, 45, 47–48

Meditatio

"At that time, John said to Jesus. . . ."

It's easy to romanticize the figure of John. Artists have depicted him leaning against the heart of Christ at the Last Supper, or gently supporting Mary at the foot of the cross. It's hard to imagine that the preacher who will one day repeat over and over, "little children, love one another," is the same man who tells Jesus in today's Gospel, ". . . we tried to prevent him because he does not follow us." Obviously John didn't always subscribe to the ideal of "love one another," but instead had an "us verses them" mentality.

We can fall into this mentality too. We can view people as not being "one of us"—those who grow up on the other side of town, or in a different ethnic group, or a different religion. Perhaps we should ask: What is it about *us* that makes us so cautious about *them?* Some people go so far as to start defining themselves in terms of their differences from others. Have you ever met someone whose working definition of Catholicism was everything that is not Protestant—or vice versa? The minute we start claiming our identity by rejecting the "other," we start to see the other as a threat.

How easily we stray from God's approach of reconciling differences: "Do not prevent him . . . whoever is not against us is for us." Yet this is not a *laissez faire* attitude that condones any and all behaviors. Jesus goes on to speak of cutting off that which leads to sin. God's plan of reconciliation has one exclusion—the exclusion of those who exclude themselves. Before the end of his life, John, the onetime "son of thunder," learned the lessons of God's love. What lesson do I need to learn today?

Oratio

Lord, you know the people I live with; you know everyone I will work with today. You know my assumptions and attitudes about them. Help me to gain a new perspective—*your* perspective. Give me your heart that looks for the best, yet does not lie about the consequences of choices and behaviors. Help me to forge strong and true relationships. Give me wisdom and compassion to truly love everyone whom I encounter and deal with today.

Contemplatio

Little children, love one another.

Twenty-Sixth Sunday of Ordinary Time— Year C

⁘· · · · · · · · · · · · ·⁘

Lectio

Luke 16:19–31

Meditatio

"And lying at his door was a poor man. . . ."

I am a woman religious and, as for any consecrated person, the words of Jesus, "sell all that you have and distribute it to the poor" (Lk 18:22), have an especially strong meaning. In today's Gospel, Jesus seems to be saying something different about money and possessions. Nowhere in these verses does God or Abraham say that the rich man should have sold all his possessions and given them away. Instead the point seems to be that the rich man should have kept his possessions and used them to take care of the beggar at his door.

The rich man finds himself in torment after death because he had not loved. How infinitely harder it would be to keep one's possessions with an open, undivided heart than to just give them away. Could I endure seeing the wealth I had earned through hard work squandered left and right on anyone who comes asking for a handout? In the parable it is the beggar covered with sores. Today it might be the immigrant, the homeless person, the displaced family, the person fleeing a natural disaster. Or it might be even closer—the brother who can't keep a job, the elderly mother who can no longer take care of herself, the daughter who has a baby to care for and no husband to help.

It is easy for our hearts to shrivel up. "I have earned this money by working hard! Let them figure out how to do it themselves." "Their situation is their own fault." "Let them learn English and find a better job." "She has no right to my money after what she has done." It takes great holiness to use money in total freedom for the sake of others and not for one's own benefit. Both those who are called to live in community and poverty and those who seek their holiness in the midst of the world are equally called to live the demanding mystery of sacrificial love.

Oratio

Come closer, Jesus, come closer. Selfishness stains my thoughts and my heart. Do not reject me for my weakness. Burn away my selfish desires and open my heart to the needs of others. Pry my hands open and make me prodigal and generous with this world's goods, that those whom I help here will welcome me into eternity. Amen.

Contemplatio

"For where your treasure is, there also will your heart be" (Lk 12:34).

Monday of the Twenty-Sixth Week of Ordinary Time

:·············:

Lectio

Luke 9:46–50

Meditatio

> *"Jesus realized the intention of their hearts. . . ."*

The apostles have been arguing about which one of them is the greatest. To counteract their ambition and pride, Jesus gives them a parable in action. He calls a little child and places him in the midst of his followers. Then he tells them this amazing truth: to receive and welcome a small child is to receive and welcome Jesus himself. And to receive and welcome Jesus is to receive and welcome the One who sent him, that is, God the Father.

The road to the Father is a road for the least among us, a road for children. What is Jesus really saying to us here? Perhaps he is telling us the reason why he came into the world as a baby. When God came to the human race as one of us, he chose to be born in a stable, to a mother unknown to the world, far from the "important" people of the day. He turned the values of the world upside down. The things that count so much in human society, count as nothing before God: money, power, prestige, fame, honor, glamour, even education. These things have their place, and we need some earthly goods to live, but Jesus warns us not to set our hearts on them.

It's a good thing God doesn't care if we've written a best seller or a hit song. Most of us will never do things like that. Children don't care about such things either. They only want to be secure in their fathers' arms, to laugh with their mothers, or to get a big hug. They're totally focused on their parents' love. A little girl who was getting used to a newly adopted younger sister was feeling a bit jealous, even though her parents made extra efforts to give her love and attention. She asked her mother one day, "If Katrina had ten mosquito bites and I had twenty, who would you take care of first?" We don't have to invent such scenarios with God, for he can take care of all of us at the same time. What delights him is the trust we show when we completely give ourselves to him.

Oratio

Jesus, you delight in the simplicity and innocence of children. I want to have a childlike heart that trusts in you completely. Free me from any fear that might hold me back. I believe in your love for me, Jesus, and I trust in you.

Contemplatio

Jesus, I offer you my heart.

Tuesday of the Twenty-Sixth Week
of Ordinary Time

⁝ · · · · · · · · · · · · ⁝

Lectio

Luke 9:51–56

Meditatio

> " . . . *he resolutely determined to journey to Jerusalem.*"

Earlier in this chapter of Luke, Jesus was transfigured before Peter, James, and John. Moses and Elijah appeared, conversing with Jesus about his "exodus." The last words that James and John heard during this incredible theophany were "This is my chosen Son; listen to him" (Lk 9:35). Now Jesus is "determined" to go to Jerusalem to accomplish his exodus. The most direct route from Galilee to Jerusalem was through Samaria. Most Jews would have avoided this route because Jews and Samaritans were bitter enemies. By entering Samaritan territory, Jesus may be prophesying the type of exodus he would accomplish. Paul characterizes it thus: "For he is our peace, he who made both one and broke down the dividing wall of enmity, through his flesh" (Eph 2:14).

But Jesus' overture is rejected, and James and John want to call down fire on the Samaritans. The resolution of this potentially fiery scene is narrated quite simply by Luke: "Jesus turned and rebuked them, and they journeyed to another village." This "rebuke" must have penetrated James and John deeply after the command they had received directly from the Father at the Transfiguration, "listen to him." And this rebuke must penetrate us deeply as well. Intolerance of others is a detour from "journeying to Jerusalem." Why? The end that the Father wishes his Son to accomplish by his "journey to Jerusalem"—his "exodus"—is peace.

This reading presents a detour in another way as well. When we cannot accomplish our plans the way we want, we often become angry like James and John. Our anger shows an inability to realize that God may be showing us what he wants through the events of our daily lives. Allowing those events to shape our journey is truly another way of "listening" to the Father.

Oratio

Jesus, I wish things would go the way I've planned them. When they don't, it must be part of the cross you invite me to take up. I have to admit, it's difficult. I can get angry so easily that I see only what went wrong. That doesn't help me see where your Father may want me to go. By wanting my own plans to be my journey to Jerusalem, I'm not following you, am I? After all, your plans didn't always work out either, did they? You know what it's like, so please inspire me the next time my plans have to change. Amen.

Contemplatio

Lord, help me journey to Jerusalem with you.

Wednesday of the Twenty-Sixth Week of Ordinary Time

∴ ············· ∴

Lectio

Luke 9:57–62

Meditatio

"But he replied. . . ."

How often do I want to respond to a new or deeper invitation from the Lord to follow him but feel that something holds me back? Maybe he wants me to follow him in greater humility, or through a more constant practice of patience. Maybe he is asking me to let go of the anxiety that can make me try to control everything, or to let go of a bad habit that impedes a more vital relationship with him. I battle with the voices that say: "I want to, but not yet." "Yes, but I've got some things pending." "Thanks for the invitation, but I need to think about it more."

Luke presents us with Jesus' personal invitation to follow him today, now! Jesus doesn't talk around his demands, but clearly tells us what discipleship will entail: living with detachment, insecurity, and the readiness for a total giving of ourselves for the sake of the kingdom. It's a large task. It's a call that demands living as Jesus did, in total dependence on the Father and in a constant readiness to go where he leads (see Mt 8:18–22).

Getting in touch with our "excuses," with the deeper reasons for holding back—such as anxiety, fear, or an exaggerated sense of responsibility—allows us to humbly place ourselves before the Lord. Then he can take our feelings and transform them into the deeper love and courage we need to step out in faith and follow where he is calling us. Otherwise our putting things off today can slowly become a lifetime of procrastination. We may end up missing out on the wonderful gifts that God is offering us through a deeper relationship with him. Has the Lord invited me to do something recently to which I have responded, "Yes Lord, but . . ."?

Oratio

Jesus, help me to recognize the beauty of your call to follow you more closely today. You may ask me to let go of things that give me comfort, pleasure, or a sense of self-satisfaction. You might invite me to relinquish a bit of my self-sufficiency and accept my need for help from you and from those around me. You might invite me to step out of my comfort zone and into situations where I can witness to you and to the Gospel. Help me accept the initial hesitation and the tug to put off my response, but then help me turn to you for strength and courage. I want to respond with a wholehearted and trust-filled "yes" so that I can grow in my relationship with you!

Contemplatio

Here I am, Lord. Send me! (see Is 6:8).

Thursday of the Twenty-Sixth Week
of Ordinary Time

❖ · · · · · · · · · · · · ❖

Lectio

Luke 10:1–12

Meditatio

> *"Jesus appointed seventy-two other disciples*
> *whom he sent ahead of him in pairs. . . ."*

Earlier in Luke's Gospel, Jesus had called twelve disciples to be with him and share his mission. He had sent them out to preach, heal, and drive out demons. More and more crowds flocked to him to hear his message of God's love and salvation and to be healed of their infirmities. His proclamation of the kingdom had drawn thousands of people who hung upon his every word. The harvest of people for the kingdom was bountiful! How was he to gather to himself the multitudes still waiting to hear the Good News?

Jesus now stands in front of seventy-two disciples whom he has just appointed. He sends them to the towns and villages on his route, to prepare the way for his coming to preach the Good News. Yet he knows these are still not enough. He tells them to pray to the Father, the Lord of the Harvest, to send even more good laborers for the harvest. He sends them and the evangelizers of all time as he himself had been sent by the Father, and he has in turn sent his twelve apostles. They are to be poor, to totally depend on God and trust in his providence. Jesus tells them to radically divest themselves of any hindrances that would weigh them down, and he instructs them on what to say and do in evangelizing. They are to bring God's peace to the people. And they are to travel in pairs. *Together*, they will support one another, advise one another, be community for each other. They have a risky mission. They have to be persons of peace if they are to give peace to those they meet.

Contemplatio

Lord Jesus, beg the Heavenly Father to send out more evangelizers! I am one of your disciples. How can I help? How can I be a person of peace in communion with my fellow members of your Church? It all depends on my relationship with you, my experience of you in my life. Your peace is not of this world. Your peace is that of accepting your gift of grace; it is the happiness and freedom of believing in you; it is spiritual security and well-being. I want to be one you send out by being a peacemaker, first in my family, then in the wider community. Awaken in me your own sense of urgency to spread the Good News of love and hope. I will look for ways of helping in my family and parish community.

Oratio

Lord, send laborers into your harvest.

Friday of the Twenty-Sixth Week
of Ordinary Time

⁘ ············· ⁘

Lectio

Luke 10:13–16

Meditatio

"Will you be exalted to heaven?"

Sometimes we might seem to live our faith almost on autopilot. It's not that we don't believe. We know we possess faith because we received that gift at Baptism. Our faith is evident because we faithfully attend Mass each Sunday. However, how have we assimilated faith into life? Is it obvious in our daily life? Today's Gospel helps us reflect on these questions. God is disappointed with the people of Chorazin and Bethsaida. Why? In both towns, Jesus had performed signs and probably miracles, yet the inhabitants failed to accept his Gospel message. "Woe to you," Jesus warns them for squandering a gift. If the cities of Tyre and Sidon, both notorious through Jewish history for their sinfulness, had heard Christ's preaching and witnessed his signs, they would have repented. Jesus is saying, in a sense, that it is better to be wicked and know it, than to be so unaware, so unconcerned with spiritual things that not even the presence and activity of the Son of Man make any difference in your life. The wicked would at least be startled into a reaction when coming face-to-face with pure goodness. They are intense and alert, up to the challenge. Jesus would not approve of their ways, but he would rejoice at their openness to change. The people who most disappoint Jesus are the uninvolved, the lukewarm. Religion is not even an issue for them. There is nothing to discuss. Signs and wonders, if noticed, are passed off as "interesting."

Lastly, Jesus rebukes the people of his own hometown, Capernaum. To them he is an upstart, someone pretending to be important. They refuse to even consider his claims. Do we take the words of Jesus seriously? Do we apply what he says to our lives? Are we spiritual minimalists? Are we doing no more than is our duty, like attending Sunday Mass, sending our children for instruction, reciting an occasional prayer? How about a sense that we have been baptized into Christ? Faith is who we are!

Oratio

Dear Lord, not one of us likes to hear your displeasure even when we merit a correction. But preserve us from the sins of indifference, smugness, and pride. These attitudes cause the soul to turn away from grace. You are ever prepared to gift us with understanding, desire, and fervor on our spiritual journey. Keep us open and eager to recognize the signs of your presence in our lives. Amen.

Contemplatio

Speak to us, Lord. We are listening.

Saturday of the Twenty-Sixth Week of Ordinary Time

:············:

Lectio

Luke 10:17–24

Meditatio

" . . . do not rejoice because the spirits are subject to you. . . ."

Luke is the only evangelist who tells us about the seventy-two disciples that Jesus sends on a mission similar to that of the Twelve. In today's Gospel, these disciples return from their tour of Galilean villages and hamlets, babbling excitedly about the miracles wrought through their words and actions. Jesus humors them for a moment, acknowledging—perhaps with tongue in cheek—that he has seen Satan falling from the sky. But then he informs the disciples that they should rejoice for a better reason. Their names have been written in heaven.

It's a matter of perspective—taking the long view for the long run. While we meet the Lord and work out our salvation with the help of his grace in the here and now, our precious present has been given to us in view of eternity. Our daily endeavors make sense only in the light of Jesus' death and resurrection and the eternal life he opened up for us. In order to keep ourselves motivated, we need to frequently gaze—or at least glance—at the larger picture.

We can gain perspective on weekends, vacations, or spiritual retreats, when we move out of our everyday lives and find it easier to see more clearly. But we don't have to wait for a break to improve our perspective. Counselors tell us that we can select almost any negative aspect of our life and view it in a more positive light by reframing it, which means seeing it in a wider context, so that it becomes smaller and less important in our eyes.

Do I have anxieties, doubts, jealousies, or resentments that I can shrink by counting my blessings?

Oratio

Jesus, Divine Master, I want to live my daily life in the light of your goodness. Help me to be grateful for the blessings of the past and present. Whenever I lose myself in the petty or the painful, I want to refocus and view the wider context. Please help me to do so. May I willingly bear whatever comes my way for love of you. I want to live in such a way that my own name will be written in heaven.

Contemplatio

"'What God has prepared for those who love him,' this God has revealed to us" (I Cor 2:9–10).

Twenty-Seventh Sunday
of Ordinary Time—Year A

⁘ · · · · · · · · · · · · ⁘

Lectio

Matthew 21:33–43

Meditatio

> *"Come, let us kill him and acquire his inheritance."*

With this parable, Jesus tells his listeners what to expect once he enters Jerusalem. The beauty of Scripture, however, is that each time we read it and pray *Lectio Divina*, God uses Scripture to reveal some truth—at times beyond the obvious point of the story—about the way we are living or should be living.

In this Gospel, the tenants show an attitude of greed. This greed goes beyond wanting only the produce that has been harvested; the tenants want to possess everything that belongs to the landowner. They fail to see all that the landowner has given them, and instead see only what they do not have. They might even think that in having it all, they will be completely happy and never have another day of tiring work. The tenants display a have-it-all attitude regardless of the means used to get it all. This have-it-all attitude is widespread in our twenty-first century mindset.

God is the landowner; we are the tenants. He has given us everything: life, health, employment, family, a place to live, food. Yet are we unhappy with what we have? Do we want a bigger house or newer car? It isn't wrong to want these things, but at what cost do we demand them? Perhaps we don't turn to dishonest methods of obtaining such things, but we may sacrifice something good for them, like our family's welfare. Do we really need it all in order to be happy? When is it enough? Do we thank God for what we do have, or do we complain about what we don't have? A grateful attitude will help us to see the little gifts in each day, including the gift of a day's work that in some way contributes to our society. Such a positive outlook enables us to see God's gifts even in the darkness.

Oratio

I thank you, Lord, for all that this day promises. Help me to see all the gifts and blessings you so lavishly give me. I know I have a choice. I can choose to see the good in this day, or I can choose to see the negative. I want to adopt your attitude, an attitude that sees every day (with its good and bad) as bathed in your love. Even the difficulties of this day will be graced with your presence to help me through them. You, Lord, are the greatest gift you give, and I thank you for the invitation to follow you.

Contemplatio

Give me the grace to see your goodness, Lord.

Twenty-Seventh Sunday
of Ordinary Time—Year B

⁝·············⁝

Lectio

Mark 10:2–16

Meditatio

> " . . . *the kingdom of God belongs to such as these.*"

Children. To us children are lovable (most of the time), and bring smiles to our faces as we play with them, watch them at their games, or even put up with their tantrums. We put children first, denying ourselves what we need to make sure a child is provided for. In Jesus' day, however, children were last. Sixty percent of children never reached adulthood. During their minor years they were on the same level as slaves. So when Jesus puts his arms around the children in a protective hug, he is sending a countercultural message. "This is what you can have if you live with the dependence of a child, counting solely on God for everything you need: intimacy with God, protection, safety, someone to look after you. This is the way I live with the Father, and I am inviting you to do the same."

It is significant that this story follows that of the Pharisees testing Jesus, trying to trip him up, refusing to believe unless he meets *their* criteria. A child would never do that. We can certainly fall into the same trap, refusing to follow Jesus' teaching because it doesn't fit our idea of right and wrong. We, too, can be hard of heart before the law of God concerning the invitation to and promise of faithfulness in covenantal love represented in the covenantal fidelity of marriage.

Jesus certainly raises the bar in this section of Mark's Gospel. It is difficult to be faithful to discipleship to Christ in the Church. I don't think it was meant to be easy. I have seen struggling people, people in broken marriages, honest sinners who are inescapably dependent on God's love and mercy in difficult situations. Though they have fallen short in keeping the law, they are "children," and thus warmly embraced by Jesus.

Oratio

God, today I pray for people whom you long to embrace, but who, for whatever reason, find it difficult to trust you with their lives. I am one of them, at least at times, but at this moment I want to remember in prayer the following persons: *(recall their names)*.

Contemplatio

I am your child, O God, and I need you in my life.

Twenty-Seventh Sunday
of Ordinary Time—Year C

:⋯⋯⋯:

Lectio

Luke 17:5–10

Meditatio

> " . . . *we have done what we were obliged to do.* . . ."

Today's Gospel goes against the grain. We're very conscious of our rights in a society where no employer can demand overtime work without giving overtime pay. The idea of being servants, and unprofitable ones at that, is completely outside of our self-concept. This Gospel seems like a put-down of honest workers. What in the world is Jesus talking about here? What is really going on? The key to this text lies in the final statement, "We are unprofitable servants." "Unmeritorious" would probably be a better translation than "unprofitable." And "servants" could also be rendered as "slaves." So we're unmeritorious slaves! That concept grates on us because we live in a culture that has made an art of entitlement. The concept of rights and privileges has been elevated over the concept of the common good. Just think of all the frivolous lawsuits that clog our courts, and the pop psychology that leads to a culture of victimhood.

Instead of making us feel good about ourselves, Jesus is giving us a dose of reality. Before God we can claim nothing.

On our own we can merit nothing. We have no rights we can assert before God, nor can we take him to court. We are nothing but humble servants, and our salvation lies in acknowledging that fact. Jesus is telling us that all our human measures have no value before God. Yet that is the good news, because if we had to rely on our own efforts to reach salvation, we would all fail miserably. Precisely because we are unmeritorious servants, Jesus suffered and died on our behalf, to merit eternal life for us. On our own, we merit nothing. But if we put our works into Jesus' hands, he transforms them into salvific deeds. We know that God will reward us for our good deeds: "And whoever gives only a cup of cold water . . . will surely not lose his reward" (Mt 10:42). But that reward is a gift, not a payment.

Oratio

Jesus, thank you for taking away the illusion that I can save myself. I offer you all the work I do for the kingdom, knowing that you will take it and multiply it like the loaves and fishes. On my own I can do nothing, but with you I can do all things. I want to do them for your love.

Contemplatio

"Let us not grow tired of doing good, for in due time we shall reap our harvest" (Gal 6:9).

Monday of the Twenty-Seventh Week of Ordinary Time

: · · · · · · · · · · · :

Lectio

Luke 10:25–37

Meditatio

> *"And who is my neighbor?"*

I heard that at least once, while on her way to receive an award, Blessed Teresa of Calcutta stopped on the sidewalk to help a needy person and missed the award ceremony! This, of course, is how the Samaritan in the parable acted. He put his plans on hold and stopped by the road to help a fellow human being.

"And who is my neighbor?" the scribe asks Jesus, probably expecting an answer that fits within his comfort zone. Instead, the learned doctor of the law finds himself immersed in a story that has a surprising protagonist. Jesus then asks *who* showed himself to be a neighbor to the robbers' victim. Not ready to admit that the hero of the tale was a Samaritan, the scribe mumbles, "The one who treated him with mercy." "Go," replies Jesus, "and do likewise." The Greek wording implies: "Do likewise constantly. Live like this."

Luke doesn't tell us what this scribe did in the end—he who had wanted to "test" Jesus. And that's fitting, because

Luke leaves the invitation open for our own response. "Live like this" means to be ready to put our plans on hold when a surprise comes our way. This is an attitude to cultivate.

During our day, we may come across someone who needs our help. But we may face other challenges, too: extra tasks because of a coworker's absence, a new assignment, a sudden illness—major or minor—assailing us or someone we love. . . . Life is filled with surprises, great and small. If we can develop an attitude of readiness, each unexpected situation will be easier to deal with. I like to picture a bird on a branch, ready to take wing at any moment.

Oratio

Lord Jesus, you are the perfect Good Samaritan, who went about doing good. Help me to be like the Samaritan in your parable, alert to the needs of others and ready to help them. I want to be ready, too, for other surprises that will require me to put my plans on hold. In our frenetic twenty-first century, it's easy to get tense when things seem to go wrong. Give me patience, Lord. Help me to be adaptable, relaxed and joyful.

Contemplatio

Live like this.

Tuesday of the Twenty-Seventh Week of Ordinary Time

∴ · · · · · · · · · · · ∴

Lectio

Luke 10:38–42

Meditatio

> *"There is need of only one thing."*

What insights can we draw for our spiritual life as we ponder today's familiar Gospel story of Jesus visiting his friends Martha and Mary? We can consider two insights that help us choose and live the "one thing" needed. First, we grow in grace and union with God in our everyday lives. Generally, God does not ask us to perform spectacular tasks or unusual penances. Rather, the opportunities to grow spiritually occur in our daily life. We find occasions to practice and grow in virtue wherever we are: home, work, a party, a sports event, a place of prayer, stuck in traffic, or on a bus. Looking back over the past day, which virtues did we have the opportunity to practice? Patience, courage, truthfulness, or humility? Gentleness, wisdom, justice, or charity? God is with us in each moment, inspiring us, offering us grace and help. Sometimes virtue seems so impossible as to be beyond us. Sometimes we don't even want to be virtuous. But if we turn to God and ask for help, he will give us the graces we need. What a gift we give to God when we try to live in this way. Then whatever we do in our daily routine becomes a living prayer.

This leads us to the second insight. Mary and Martha are doing very different things. Mary is listening to Jesus while Martha is preparing and serving the meal. But they have in common good intentions, for they are both acting out of love. We, too, can strive to do things out of love for God and others. Love is not a feeling, but a choice to act or not act. Out of love, we choose to be patient, to help someone, or to take a walk. Let love be the fundamental reason for our choices. This is the key to holiness, peace, and happiness.

Oratio

Jesus, when I hear again your words to Martha, "There is need of only one thing," it gives me pause. I get so caught up in the busyness of the day that I sometimes forget that my everyday life is where I am called to become holy. I forget the sacredness of each moment and each action. Enable me to remember this today, Lord. Help me turn to you in the challenges and difficulties that I will encounter, so that I can grow in whatever virtues I will need. Grant me an increase in charity so that I do all with love. Amen.

Contemplatio

You are here with me, Lord. I do this for you.

Wednesday of the Twenty-Seventh Week of Ordinary Time

⋱············⋰

Lectio

Luke 11:1–4

Meditatio

> *"Lord, teach us to pray. . . ."*

Some people wonder whether conversation is fast becoming a lost art in this digital age of social networking, emoticons, and texting. It's being replaced by an unedited stream of consciousness. This is true in some quarters, perhaps, but not for long. We have a built-in craving for deep human connection. With life as it is, though, we sense that we often don't know how to connect with others, especially with God. "Lord, *teach* us to pray."

Oh, we can manage well enough without prayer. Even two thousand years ago, working as a fisherman or tax collector didn't require a course in contemplation. But the ache for relationship with God still flourishes in the human heart. This is a God whom Jesus knows intimately—in the Temple, on a hillside, in the early hours of morning, and as he heals the sick or blesses bread. The pull and possibility of this intimacy is not lost on his own. One of his disciples speaks for them all: "Lord, teach *us* to pray."

The disciple calls Jesus "Lord," and so, as Luke implies, one person's request becomes the cry of every heart through the ages. Jesus brings us into relationship with the God he knows as Father: "When you pray, say: Father. . . ." This relationship is not just a command; Jesus won it for us when he gave himself for us into the Father's hands. Such a prayer that receives and offers forgiveness heals any experience of father other than Godlike fatherhood. Jesus shares with us his own power to forgive and heal. *"Lord, teach us to pray."* This is our daily bread; it sustains and delights us and others, whenever we share it—like the Eucharist. What a school of prayer! The Eucharist's source and summit of life is also the font and fullness of communion with God. May it transform who we are into a continuous act of praise, a liturgy of life. "Lord, teach us to *pray*."

Oratio

Lord, I want my prayer to be deep and satisfying, but I'm so inconstant in cultivating a prayerful spirit. If it's true that we live as we pray, it also seems that we pray as we live. Help me slow down a little today. Tomorrow I'll probably say the same thing—and that's good. You told us, "If you ask anything of me in my name, I will do it" (Jn 14:14). Lord, I'm holding you to your promise! I'll try again to keep mine.

Contemplatio

"Lord, teach us to pray."

Thursday of the Twenty-Seventh Week of Ordinary Time

:⋯⋯⋯⋯:

Lectio

Luke 11:5–13

Meditatio

". . . the Father in Heaven . . ."

Jesus is praying with his disciples gathered around. They may be resting, thinking, or looking at nature, but they are there with Jesus, who is absorbed in communion with his Father. Perhaps it is when Jesus turns back to join them, and they see the peace and joy on his face, that they ask for what any one of us would have wanted in the same circumstances: "Lord, teach us to pray."

Jesus teaches them the Our Father, and leaves us the most precious words ever to fall on human ears. But Jesus wants to make sure that we know what is involved in those deceptively simple petitions. So in the next two long paragraphs he illustrates this wondrous relationship between God and us. Jesus shows us the dispositions of God, our Father and faithful Friend, who is always ready to be there for us at any hour of any day. He uses words that are almost an oath: "And I tell you, ask . . . seek . . . knock." Jesus wants us to know what a great power over his heart the Heavenly Father has given to us, how willing the Father is to bend to us and hear our prayers for enlightenment, assistance, salvation, and yes, daily bread.

It seems that Jesus wants us to realize that the words we say are not as important as the trusting love that brings us to ask, seek, knock, and come close to the Father who has created us all as his children. Sometimes I am so distracted and tired when I pray that I can hear myself almost babbling as I present my petitions, and I'm a bit ashamed that I wasn't able to pray better. But prayer is a relationship, and the words overflow from the love and trust in that joining of hearts, God's and mine.

Oratio

Good Father in Heaven, I can never thank you enough for sending your Son, Jesus, who has revealed your image in his love-filled life and redeeming death. Give me the grace to see your ever-present love and care in all the events of my daily life. Encouraged by Jesus' advice, I will ask, seek, and knock at the door of your Fatherly heart. I trust you will give me your Spirit so that I can resemble you as your child, and grow in love every day.

Contemplatio

Our Father, my Father.

Friday of the Twenty-Seventh Week of Ordinary Time

∴ · · · · · · · · · · · · ∴

Lectio

Luke 11:15–26

Meditatio

> *"But if it is by the finger of God that I drive out demons,*
> *then the Kingdom of God has come upon you."*

A woman in her fifties was an alcoholic without a job. She was heartbroken. I met her on a retreat, where she told me her story, and I prayed with her. We went back in prayer to the place in her life that needed the most healing: the birth of her first child. Her daughter had been taken away from her because she was "not suited to be a mother." She was in her teens, unwed, afraid. She was never allowed to see her daughter, or the two children born after that. Now, almost forty years later, she still bore the scars of the shame and sorrow.

In prayer she took Jesus' hand and returned to the hospital where she had given birth to her daughter. She remembered what was happening around her, words people said, what she felt. Then she stopped and observed Jesus looking at her with such compassion and love. When her daughter was born, he took her from the doctor's hands with joy, raised her in the air and blessed his Father for her birth. Then he laid the child next to my friend. For the first time she "saw" her baby. Then I told her to wait because Jesus would say something just for her to hear. Jesus spoke healing words to her, words that swept away the demons of shame that had possessed her. "You are a good mother," he told her. I gently started to cry, moved at Jesus' goodness to her. A year later I met my friend again on retreat. She had a job, was attending A.A. meetings, and had met her three children, who had come searching for their mother.

The kingdom of God is nothing more than the presence of Jesus among us. It is not in the future or in the past, something far away, or only inside a sanctuary. Jesus is here and now for you and me, wherever we are. He still sweeps away the demons that possess us and weigh us down with shame and sorrow. Jesus is God-for-us.

Oratio

In the name of Jesus, may the kingdom of light and love shine in our darkness and turn our nights into days, our fears into hope, our hatred into love. Let the kingdom of God arise where once there were shame and sorrow, so that our earthly life will receive a new form as we await the day we will enjoy eternal life forever. Amen.

Contemplatio

Jesus, heal the darkest place of my life.

Saturday of the Twenty-Seventh Week of Ordinary Time

∴ · · · · · · · · · · · · ∴

Lectio

Luke 11:27–28

Meditatio

"Rather, blessed are those who hear the word of God and observe it."

It is telling that Jesus redirects the compliments of the woman in the crowd who cries out, "Blessed is the womb that carried you and the breasts at which you nursed." These are very particular blessings of the Mother of God, while also being an indirect compliment to Jesus himself. But the blessing is exclusive, and may give us the impression that we cannot share in the blessedness of Mary and Jesus. That is not the Good News Jesus came to bring. As the Way that leads us to the Father, Jesus desires to bless all God's people, leading everyone who will follow him into this state of "blessedness." Ultimately, Jesus did not come for the privilege of a few, but for the salvation of many.

Keeping this reality in mind, we can see that Jesus' exchange with the woman in the crowd reveals the deepest source of Mary's blessedness. At the Annunciation, Mary heard the word of the Lord and responded immediately, with complete surrender. Her whole life is one of faith in action.

Each of us shares with Mary this opportunity to become blessed through our own response of faith.

With Mary as model and guide, Jesus invites us to hear the word of God and observe it. We are invited to the obedience of the sons and daughters of God. The word "obedience" comes from the Latin root, *oboedire*, which means "to listen." We cannot obey if, through silent contemplation of Christ's words and actions, we have not first taken the time to hear and understand what is being asked. But even this is not enough. We must also allow that word to confront our lives, with a willingness to make concrete changes based on the invitations we receive. This kind of change takes real courage and perseverance—it requires a ready and willing heart.

Oratio

Mary, our Mother, in your earthly life, you were a woman of profound listening. You pondered in your heart all the words and actions of your Son and allowed their mystery to permeate your being. Through your obedience to his word, you became an instrument of divine grace for the world. Teach me, your child, how to listen to your Son and respond to his word in my life. Obtain for me the grace of an obedient heart that receives the word of God with a deep readiness to go wherever it will lead, and a true willingness to make any changes it may require.

Contemplatio

Let it be done to me according to your Word.

Twenty-Eighth Sunday of Ordinary Time—Year A

∴∙∙∙∙∙∙∙∙∙∙∙∙∙∴

Lectio

Matthew 22:1–12

Meditatio

> " . . . come to the feast."

Each of us can put ourselves into this parable because God invites each of us to the same wedding feast. God does not invite us only once. He continually invites us throughout our lives. At various times we either have or have not accepted God's invitations. Like those in the parable who do not accept the invitation, we affect others when we choose not to accept. Sometimes, we don't accept the invitation because our priorities lie elsewhere: our own interests, our own will, our personal needs. By choosing ourselves over God, we begin to break our bond with him. We gradually refuse God himself. This leads to breaking our bonds with everyone else who is being invited as well.

Unfortunately, we may also react violently to those who bear God's invitation. God sends us his invitation in many different situations and through many people: parents, guardians, children, siblings, coworkers, neighbors. When we react violently, we rupture the common relationship we share with all others who are invited to the wedding. Rather than being in communion with others, we literally dwell in isolation.

Many of us live in a state of continual rupture and isolation in our daily lives. This reality will not change unless we can sincerely ask ourselves, "What keeps me from accepting God's invitation to go to the wedding banquet he is preparing for me?" We will never be truly happy or at peace until we can accept God's invitation and go to the wedding feast. Our isolation will then be transformed into the bliss of one who has been chosen to participate in the celebration of life.

Oratio

Jesus, thank you for telling us this story. I realize that I too am a participant in this story that is being lived out right now in my daily life. At times I am blinded to this reality because I am preoccupied with my own concerns. Help me to see beyond my preoccupations and realize that in every moment you are extending an invitation to join you at your wedding. This reality alone must motivate all my choices. Grant me the ability to accept your Father's invitation in every moment of my life, Jesus. Amen.

Contemplatio

Yes, Father, I accept your invitation. I will come to your Son's wedding.

Twenty-Eighth Sunday of Ordinary Time— Year B

⁑· · · · · · · · · · · ·⁑

Lectio

Mark 10:17–30

Meditatio

> *"Jesus, looking at him, loved him. . . ."*

The man in today's Gospel asks Jesus, "What must I do to inherit eternal life?" Yet when Jesus tells him to "sell what you have and give to the poor," the man walks away sad, because "he had many possessions." But why did he just walk away? Why didn't he ask Jesus for clarification? Why didn't Jesus call him back and ask for an explanation? Herein is the mystery of freedom. God never forces himself on us, but leaves us free to choose. The man in our Gospel is looking for a deeper relationship with God. Is he so attached to his possessions that he can't see his life without them? Jesus invites him to live not so much in calculating what he should not be doing (stealing, killing, lying . . .) but rather in how he can help the poor, those less fortunate than himself. Yet, he just walks away.

Even more striking is the phrase that Jesus looked at him with love. What does he see in this person? Whatever it is, it moves Jesus to invite him to be a close follower. As we contemplate the word of God, Jesus looks at us with love.

He extends this invitation to us also. Jesus wants us to share in his relationship with the Father. Through our Baptism we have already been brought into this awesome relationship. We are sons and daughters of God. The Gospels reveal how Jesus lived this relationship. He was constantly aware of the Father's presence and addressed his prayer to the Father. Jesus was vigilant for the poor, the hungry, the sick, and the imprisoned. And we know how the Father regards the Son: "This is my beloved son . . ." (Mt 17:5). Jesus is our example for everything. We don't have to forge our own way in life. If the Father asks me to trust, he has given me Jesus as my example. If he asks me to love others, he has given Jesus as my example.

Oratio

Lord Jesus, look on me with love. Thank you for restoring my relationship with the Father, making me a child of God. Jesus, you are my brother, the Way between the Father and me. I offer you all and await all from you. Jesus, Way of Sanctity, make me your faithful imitator. Jesus, render me perfect as the Father who is in heaven. Jesus, live in me, so that I may live in you, and do not permit me to separate myself from you. Grant that I may live eternally in the joy of your love.

Contemplatio

By myself I can do nothing, but with God I can do all things.

Twenty-Eighth Sunday of Ordinary Time—Year C

:·············:

Lectio

Luke 17:11–19

Meditatio

> " . . . realizing he had been healed,
> returned, glorifying God in a loud voice. . . ."

In Jesus' day, having leprosy, a highly contagious disease of the skin, meant virtual exile. Separated from family, shunned by the community, the leper could hope to be reintegrated with society and his or her family only by being healed. So when these ten lepers spot Jesus from a distance, they all call out to him, begging for his merciful and miraculous healing. Jesus complies, healing them physically and restoring them to their families and communities.

Sin does in an inward way what leprosy does externally. The effects of sin touch not only the person who commits the sin, but also everyone in the community. This raises a barrier separating the sinner from the community. An act of selfishness on our part begets other sins. My sin toward one person can affect how that person will react later. In other words, my sin doesn't harm only me. It harms the whole community, almost like invisible tentacles clutching at others' hearts.

In the Gospel account, Jesus heals all ten victims of leprosy. I am sure that all of them are happy to be healed, but only one returns to give thanks. He recognizes Jesus as the source of his healing and restoration. The Gospel text even suggests that the man approaches Jesus shouting his joyful praise to God. God offers us the same healing and restoration through the sacrament of Reconciliation. In it God tells us, "I forgive you and I want to heal you. Please don't separate yourself from me—I love you." The words of absolution are words of restoration and love. As someone reminded me recently, God is not waiting for me so that he can wag his finger at me in disappointment. Whether we receive the sacrament or simply examine our conscience, God opens his arms wide to embrace us and bring us back to communion and community.

Oratio

With what joy, Lord, I should run to a reconciliatory encounter with you as your pure love washes over me. Afterward I fall to my knees in total, unashamed gratitude for the love you pour out. I pray today for the grace to turn to you in sincerity with all that I have done, both the good and the not so good. May I give them all to you, so as to praise you for the good and receive your forgiveness for what is not so good. Help me to avoid the sins I am most prone to commit again—I want to be wholly yours today and always.

Contemplatio

"In the shadow of your wings I shout for joy" (Ps 63:8).

Monday of the Twenty-Eighth Week of Ordinary Time

⁝·············⁝

Lectio

Luke 11:29–32

Meditatio

" . . . no sign will be given it, except the sign of Jonah."

As I read the Gospel of Luke, I see that in this section Jesus is speaking to various groups of people. In fact, "still more people" are gathering to hear him, so I join the crowd and listen to what he has to say. It seems that this crowd seeks signs too, just like the people where I come from. Besides that, Jesus is saying that the pagan city of Nineveh was more receptive to God's prophet than this generation is now. Even more, "there is something greater than Jonah here." Jonah walked through Nineveh and preached repentance. He who is "greater than Jonah" lived, preached, died, and rose from the dead. Am I listening? The conversion of pagan Nineveh is one reality. The victory won for us in God's Son is quite another. A whole new reality has dawned upon the world in Christ.

God has sent his Son, and this marks the beginning of a new age that cannot be conquered, dimmed, or dismissed. It's a new reality with a capital R. God is the measure of everything. All of us have our origin in him. All of us will return to him, to render an account of our lives. In this new era, however, we need not go alone. We have the Beloved Son with us. We are to be marked by his sign: his passion, death, and resurrection. That is how the Father will recognize Christ in us. We are to be a people who, in a very real way, are his own, a people of hope. We follow one "greater than Jonah"; one who walked through death into life. We are to be a people of hope because we know that earthly life, goods, and signs are not the final end. More, much more, awaits us. The "much more" is the sign of Jonah given today. We are Christ's body, to be his hands and feet today, offering hope to each person and circumstance we encounter.

Oratio

Father, in giving us Christ, you have given us everything. Saint Paul tells us that in your Son every "spiritual blessing" is ours. Help me understand the depth of what you have done for all generations in giving us your Son. I seek so many things, chasing after bubbles, but in Christ I have more than enough. Thank you for giving us your Beloved Son, teaching us all we need for real fulfillment through him. Thank you for Jesus, who is "greater than Jonah" and calls me to be a sign with him.

Contemplatio

Make me a sign of life and hope to those with whom I work today.

Tuesday of the Twenty-Eighth Week of Ordinary Time

⁘ · · · · · · · · · · · · ⁘

Lectio

Luke 11:37–41

Meditatio

> *"Give alms, and . . . everything will be clean for you."*

Even though the evangelists don't mention it, Jesus and the Pharisees must have had some common ground. For example, they often invited him to dinner. At one such dinner, Jesus praised a woman who kissed his feet and anointed them with oil. His host had neglected the customary signs of welcome.

In today's passage, too, a minor confrontation develops, and Jesus states that inner purity is more important than outward cleanliness. Luke adds a phrase that the other evangelists don't use: Jesus' host will be cleansed inwardly if he gives alms.

Almsgiving is important in the Jewish and Christian religions. The Book of Sirach states that almsgiving is a sacrifice of praise (see 35:2). Matthew quotes Jesus as saying, "And whoever gives only a cup of cold water . . . will surely not lose his reward" (10:42). Saint Paul took up a collection from the mainly Gentile churches to aid the poor Hebrew Christians in Jerusalem.

Contributing to a worthy cause helps us feel good. We're participating in an effort larger than ourselves. Often the small gifts of many people are the only way a project can be realized. We can make a difference!

For most people in our culture, making monetary contributions is part of life. So when we consider growth in almsgiving, it may be more helpful to reflect on some of its other forms—the sharing of time and talent, the offering of prayers and sacrifices. We can ask ourselves whether we can do more without neglecting our primary responsibilities. For some, the answer will be *yes*.

What's *your* response?

Oratio

Jesus, you became poor for our sakes, so that we might become rich. Teach me how to be poor in spirit and a cheerful giver. Guide me as I reflect on the various forms of giving. Inspire me to choose those ways of contributing to the works of the Church and/or helping my sisters and brothers that are best suited to my possibilities. Inspire me to offer *what* I can and *when* I can. If my giving ought to remain focused on my own household or community, please help me to understand that and act accordingly.

Contemplatio

"It is more blessed to give than to receive" (Acts 20:35).

Wednesday of the Twenty-Eighth Week
of Ordinary Time

∴ · · · · · · · · · · · ∴

Lectio

Luke 11:42–46

Meditatio

"These you should have done, without overlooking the others."

Sometimes I get so caught up in details that I miss the big picture. This can be helpful when I need to focus. But it can also be a problem if I'm so focused that I miss the opportunities to serve others that God shows me right now. Jesus is talking about this with the Pharisees and scholars of the Law. In this instance they are following the law of paying certain tithes, but are not giving attention to the greatest commandment of all, love for God.

In building a house, the interior design is important, but the foundation and walls have to be put up first! If the foundation is not solid, then the rest of the house cannot stand. Jesus acknowledges that tithes should be paid, but we can't overlook the most important laws: love of God and neighbor. Sometimes the good that we choose to do can be self-serving and lead us to rely on ourselves. Jesus offers us the joy and strength to follow his way of surrender to the Father in self-giving love. It is a matter of tuning in to the heart of God and trying to live and love with God's heart.

Our day is full of moments in which we need to discern our priorities. What should I give my attention to now? Am I cramming too many events, meetings, and projects into my schedule? Am I losing sight of the big picture? Discernment helps us look at our daily tasks with a desire to truly do what God desires. I can get into a routine of doing a lot of good and productive things, but then lose sight of God's call in my life to be a servant and lover of humanity. When I lose sight of what God is calling me to, I can end up following my own way, doing the things that seem most important, without truly seeing what is important to God. But, through daily prayer, I can stay in tune with God and the needs of the world around me.

Oratio

Jesus, thank you for reminding me of the greatest commandments of all—love for God and neighbor. In the midst of my busy day, help me to continuously notice your movements in me and your call to be a servant. Help me to notice the needs of those around me throughout the day and to respond with a great and selfless love. Thank you for your love for me and for calling me to love.

Contemplatio

Here I am, O Lord. I come to do your will (see Heb 10:7).

Thursday of the Twenty-Eighth Week of Ordinary Time

:・・・・・・・・・・・・・:

Lectio

Luke 11:47–54

Meditatio

> *" . . . the key of knowledge. . . ."*

Today's Gospel focuses on the woes that Jesus pronounces against the scribes and Pharisees. In reading this text, we realize that he is acting in the biblical tradition of prophetic denunciation of evil. Jesus' intent is not to condemn all the people of Israel, not even all the Pharisees. His intent is to highlight an error in order to draw people away from it. He's acting like a doctor who has to administer some painful remedy to cure the patient.

Jesus speaks of how the prophets were killed when they announced God's word. He then says, "You have taken away the key of knowledge." In this context, knowledge seems to refer to access to the kingdom of God. "You yourselves did not enter and you stopped those trying to enter." In the Bible, the symbol of keys indicates authority. Jesus is saying that the religious leaders blocked people from entering the kingdom instead of helping them to get in. It's like a teacher who, instead of helping students prepare to pass an important exam, deliberately tries to make them fail.

The prophets were rejected and killed by people who didn't want to hear their sometimes harsh messages. The key of knowledge is humility of heart, the ability to accept a truthful message even when it's hard to hear. Resistance to truth, as well as its acceptance, come more from our heart than our mind. That is why God sent John the Baptist to prepare the way for Christ. Unlike the religious professionals, John came on the scene with no credentials except the intensity of his love. He pointed to Jesus, not himself, saying, "He must increase; I must decrease" (Jn 3:30). John, the voice in the wilderness, preached a baptism of repentance to prepare people to accept Jesus. John gave the key of knowledge to those who would accept it. Today, the world is filled with many conflicting voices. But the voice of Jesus teaching through the Church is loud and clear. Which voice am I going to listen to?

Oratio

Jesus, you give us the key of knowledge, the key to entering the kingdom of heaven. Help me to have true humility of heart, so that I may listen attentively to your teaching and accept it fully.

Contemplatio

Lord, I want to listen to your voice.

Friday of the Twenty-Eighth Week
of Ordinary Time

:⋯⋯⋯⋯:

Lectio

Luke 12:1–7

Meditatio

> ". . . whatever you have said in the darkness
> will be heard in the light. . . ."

So often in the Gospels, Jesus points out the hypocrisy of some of the religious leaders. In fact, sometimes we can become so used to it that we become deaf to the concern Jesus has for us. Let's take the word "hypocrisy" and translate it into a term often used today: "transparency." Companies and parishes must have financial transparency. Leaders have to be transparent and put into full view their motivations and the information that has led to their decisions. We want our elected officials to be transparent. Transparency as honesty is valued as a virtue in children, and also in adults.

Those who demand the most transparency in others are often the least transparent about their own activities and decisions. Their demand for transparency may just be a politically correct term for expressing their feelings of being marginalized and not included. Or perhaps they are rebellious against authority. Such persons act hypocritically, demanding transparency of others but refusing to be honest themselves.

Yet other people are honest and transparent. How do we reverence transparency in others when they make themselves vulnerable by revealing motivations, desires, weaknesses, dreams, or decisions? Their transparency must be respected by those who are entrusted with valuable and sensitive information. This takes maturity, which sometimes others lack. Then the person being open and honest may be betrayed and hurt because others cannot be transparent themselves. In situations like this, some of Jesus' sayings can bring comfort to us: "There is nothing concealed that will not be revealed . . . do not be afraid of those who kill the body. . . . Even the hairs of your head have all been counted. Do not be afraid. You are worth more than many sparrows."

Oratio

Jesus, so many misunderstandings have made my life complex. But you know the truth. You know I've tried. You know my weaknesses, and you are here in the mess. You are making me holy in the pain of betrayal. I hear you repeat over and over, "Do not be afraid." I open my heart completely to your gaze, and hide nothing from you. Amen.

Contemplatio

Light in the darkness, shine in my soul.

Saturday of the Twenty-Eighth Week of Ordinary Time

⁘··············⁘

Lectio

Luke 12:8–12

Meditatio

> *"For the Holy Spirit will teach you*
> *at that moment what you should say."*

As we near the end of the liturgical year, the readings of the liturgy become more serious, even foreboding. Most of us will probably never be brought before rulers or authorities in the way the Gospel describes. But if we think about it, our Christian convictions are on trial every day of our lives. Small personal struggles, known only to ourselves, test our love and keep us praying for the promised grace and strength of the Holy Spirit.

Besides that, we are asked to take part in the battles of our own day, to proclaim the truth of the Gospel even in the face of what society considers "politically correct." Judeo-Christian values are constantly challenged; unjust laws exist in our own nation. We must allow ourselves to be the voice of the living word. Sometimes we may be called to actually use our physical voice, but even if our words are ignored, our example is a silent word. As the proverb says, "Actions speak louder than words."

Crucial life and death struggles are going on all over the globe. They may take place far away, but they are still very real. The Church still has martyrs who are undergoing persecution in many countries. The odds seem stacked against us, but we must heed the living word in today's Gospel. Every age has its own struggles, but God always defends us if we let the Holy Spirit lead us. We look beyond the visible scene with the eyes of faith, for we know that the war has already been won on Calvary. Confidence in our Lord's love is the key to true wisdom. The victory will always be Jesus Christ's.

Oratio

O Lord, be my light in the darkness of this world. Guide my steps with your word and fill my mind with your truth. Enlarge my heart with your love and grant me the courage to witness to you in every situation. Use me to bring your love to others. I accept that I may not always understand *how* you are using me, but I trust that one day, in this life or the next, you will reveal it to me. I only know that by simply living my daily life according to your word, you *will* use me. Keep my eyes fixed on you. Increase my faith. From eternity to eternity, you are God.

Contemplatio

I am yours, Lord. May my life speak of you.

Twenty-Ninth Sunday of Ordinary Time— Year A

:·············:

Lectio

Matthew 22:15–21

Meditatio

> *". . . repay to Caesar what belongs to Caesar. . . ."*

They want to put Jesus on the spot, but of course he knows better than to fall into the trap. The census tax is paid by women and men from the ages of twelve and fourteen, respectively, to sixty-five. It is unpopular with the extreme nationalists, but not with the Herodians, who are in league with the Romans. So if Jesus says that the tax is lawful, he would displease the nationalists, but to say the opposite would displease both the Romans and the Herodians. His answer is so simple and clear that no one could contest it. Moreover, it reminds his listeners that they have duties not only to Caesar, but also to God. It's interesting that the inscription on most of the coins collected for the tax was: "Tiberius Caesar, august son of the divine Augustus, high priest." Clearly, Jesus couldn't have endorsed that inscription, so this shows that we don't need to contest every claim of Caesar that we don't agree with.

But we do have to remember—and pass on to younger generations—the basic truth that legality and morality aren't always the same. For example, the Ten Commandments forbid killing other humans, including the unborn. The commandments don't say anything about wild animals. Where my religious community lives, wild animals are protected by law unless they harm someone. And abortion is legal. Recently one of our sisters commented that the human being may be the only species in our state that isn't legally protected at all stages of life.

Yet some issues are less clear-cut. Fortunately, help regarding moral issues is available whenever we need it. The Web sites of the bishops conference and individual dioceses often address these issues. For basic principles, we have the teachings of the Holy Father, which can be accessed in print or on the Web. When it comes to making our personal decisions, we can consult a priest—for example, when we approach the sacrament of Reconciliation. The availability of such guidance is a real blessing.

Oratio

Jesus, Divine Master, I thank you for giving us the Church to lead and guide us. How many of our contemporaries don't have access to such secure moral teaching! When I need to understand an issue that's unclear, I intend to take the time to research it. This way, besides acquiring an informed conscience for myself, I'll be able to help others if the need or opportunity arises.

Contemplatio

" . . . and to God what belongs to God."

Twenty-Ninth Sunday of Ordinary Time—Year B

∴ · · · · · · · · · · · · ∴

Lectio

Mark 10:35–45

Meditatio

> *"For the Son of Man did not come to be served*
> *but to serve and to give his life as a ransom for many."*

James and John *thought* they knew what they wanted. Along with Peter, they had witnessed the transfiguration of Jesus and seen his glory. Perhaps they sensed the privileged place of this revelation and, being human, they longed to lay claim to this place of honor more permanently in the kingdom of God. They had witnessed the healings Jesus performed, and they had seen him calm storms at sea and walk on water. Despite the Lord's repeated predictions of his passion, they consistently mistook the place of power in Christ's mission of self-offering and love. The reality of a suffering Messiah who would choose to completely empty himself rather than take up his reign in power was far beyond their human expectations. But can we blame them, knowing our own personal quests for honor and power?

As Jesus prepares to go to Jerusalem where he will drink his cup to the dregs, I can only imagine the pain in his heart. Like each of us, he must have longed for the support and understanding of his friends. He has tried to prepare their minds and hearts for the suffering to come. Perhaps with this latest request, he finds himself wondering if they have heard him at all. . . . How many times has he tried to tell them that true greatness is found in humble service? Yet he remains patient—the living icon of the humble, gentle Master who did not come to be served, but to serve.

"Can you drink the cup . . . ?" The words of Jesus echo in my heart today. If we take this invitation seriously, we will come to understand the ardent desire of the Master who longs for us to live life fully with him. He invites us to look lovingly into this cup he holds out to us . . . to examine the contents along with our hearts so as to be able to answer "yes" with our whole being.

Oratio

Jesus, you fully accepted the cup the Father gave you to drink, and you drank it to the last drop. You gave your "yes" fully and completely, knowing well you were being asked to drink the depths of all the joys and sufferings of the human race. As I gaze into this cup that you hold out to me, give me the courage to embrace fully all that is there—the joy and the sorrow, the beautiful and the difficult, the celebration and the suffering. Give me the grace to live my life fully for you so that my life, too, might become a gift of love poured out for others.

Contemplatio

Make me a living tabernacle of your love.

Twenty-Ninth Sunday of Ordinary Time—
Year C

⁝· · · · · · · · · · · ·⁝

Lectio

Luke 18:1–8

Meditatio

> " . . . pray always without becoming weary."

How can a person "pray always"? Don't we need to go about our daily lives, fulfilling our obligations, using our mind to its full potential? If we are occupied, how can we "pray always"? Jesus is not suggesting that we spend all our time in prayer. Instead, he is encouraging us to pray, to keep on going, and to nurture our relationship with him even when we feel weary. We don't want to give up on God, because he never gives up on us and pursues us as a smitten lover would. We don't want to let shame lead us away from God, because he loves us unconditionally. We don't want to turn away from God, because he doesn't turn his back on us and is always gently guiding our eyes toward him.

When we find prayer to be easy, we imagine never giving it up. But when we come to rocky and tumultuous times of prayer, it is difficult to sustain conversation with God. Yet the saints and mystics unanimously urge us never to lose heart. We need to persevere even when we feel nothing, when we are angry at God, when we are bored, and when our interests pull us in an entirely different direction. Through it all, we must not grow weary but remain faithful to prayer, convinced of God's unfailing love and fidelity. Prayer can take many forms, whether it is the prayer of the Church (liturgical prayer) or private devotion. Our prayer may be long, or it may consist of brief conversations with the Lord. We can raise our hearts to praise God for a grace received, for the beauty of creation, or to ask for favors. We can pray for ourselves, and we can bring to God the needs of others. Above all, we may always ask God to give us the gift of prayer—the gift of enjoying a familiar, loving, and grateful relationship with him.

Oratio

Lord God, may you be praised for the beauty of dawn and sunset. Lord God, help those people who are suffering due to natural disasters. Lord God, grant that my family may be safe. Lord God, I love you and praise you! Amen.

Contemplatio

"Whoever remains in me and I in him will bear much fruit, because without me you can do nothing" (Jn 15:5).

Monday of the Twenty-Ninth Week of Ordinary Time

∴∴∴∴∴∴∴∴∴∴∴

Lectio

Luke 12:13–21

Meditatio

> " . . . one's life does not consist of possessions."

Some scripture scholars think that Luke's Gospel and the Acts of the Apostles were written for Gentile Christians, in particular Christian communities struggling with equity among the haves and have-nots. Today's passage is about greed and wanting to keep what we view as "ours." Interestingly, Jesus doesn't say that we should get rid of all our possessions. Instead, Jesus points out that neither the quantity nor the quality of possessions should define the quality of one's life.

Jesus is speaking about the difference between possessing "things" and being possessed by them. The former points to an inner freedom, while the latter points to a kind of slavery. In this parable, the man is a fool not because he is rich, but because he hoards his belongings; he is a slave to "having." We too can fall victim to our possessions. We become slaves to them when we are overly concerned about them and cannot openly share our things or give them away. The slave to possessions thinks, "What is mine is mine and no one can take it away." If a possession "owns" us, we are no longer free to give it up. That possession can be as big as a car, as small as a piece of jewelry, or as inexpensive as a baseball card; it can even be all of those things combined. To hold onto these things with a tight fist is to have one's life consist of possessions. The invitation to all Christians is to have some possessions and to enjoy them, but not to let them become the goal in one's life. Rather, all that we have—whether we are considering nature, people, or possessions, are gifts received from God. We must allow this parable to question us about our possessions. Do we own them, or do they own us?

Oratio

The only thing I want or really need, Lord, is you. I ask that you possess me. As I look around where I am sitting and praying, I take a moment to really see all you have given me. Help me to loosen my grip on those things that I am holding tightly. You, Lord, and not things, are the source of my happiness. Thank you, Lord, for all the graces you have already given me, and thank you for all those that will continue to come for the rest of this day. Amen.

Contemplatio

Lord, you are all I need.

Tuesday of the Twenty-Ninth Week of Ordinary Time

⁝ · · · · · · · · · · · · ⁝

Lectio

Luke 12:35–38

Meditatio

> *" . . . when he comes and knocks. . . ."*

It's not a matter of *if*—it's a matter of *when* and *how*. In one sense God never leaves us alone. He sustains all things in existence with his creative love. Through Baptism and the other sacraments he is present in his sanctifying grace. The gift of faith-hope-love is freely given to us. It is meant to be unwrapped, opened, used, treasured, and shown to others. In another sense, however, God does "leave" us. In our limited human nature, we quickly lose track of God's presence. God is always with us—but we are not always with him. The cares and concerns of day-to-day living barge in and claim our attention. The people we live with need our love shown in concrete ways: providing food, making beds, running errands . . . doing a thousand and one things in mundane moments of choices, words, and actions.

The ideal exhortation of today's Gospel, "Blessed are those servants whom the master finds vigilant on his arrival," may seem out of reach. But then we remember Jesus telling us elsewhere in the Gospel that he considers as given to him the acts of kindness we extend to the "least" among us. The Christian vocation is lived out in service to others, after the pattern of Jesus Christ. He gave himself on the cross for our salvation and continues to give himself in the Eucharist.

Heaven is sometimes called the wedding feast of the Lamb of God. It is the celebration of the union of human and divine in Jesus Christ. It is God's feast of life—eternal life—bestowed upon his creatures. In the Eucharist, this wedding feast becomes present in our daily lives. Truly God is already in our midst serving us! He comes and knocks on our hearts, asking us to enter into his banquet of life. He comes and knocks on our doors in the "least" of those whom we encounter in our daily journeys.

Oratio

Jesus, you come fresh from the wedding banquet of heaven; you knock on my door this morning and ask to enter into my day. Come, Lord, come into my heart. Come into my thoughts. Come into my choices. Teach me how to serve you present in my brothers and sisters. You already know the people and the situations I will encounter. Walk with me so those whom I meet today will find your compassion and strength in my words and actions. Show me in turn how to be a gracious guest at your table.

Contemplatio

Eucharist—God is already in our midst serving us!

Wednesday of the Twenty-Ninth Week of Ordinary Time

⋮ · · · · · · · · · · · ⋮

Lectio

Luke 12:39–48

Meditatio

" . . . *for at an hour you do not expect, the Son of Man will come. . . .*"

In today's Gospel, Jesus may seem as if he is giving advice to homeowners on safety measures and security, but actually he is speaking about being prepared. Jesus is readying his listeners, not for disaster, but for a time of rejoicing—in fact, for the greatest moment of their lives. The kingdom is coming! The Master will return at a time we can't know. We can anticipate it, however, and this is what Jesus is advising his followers to do. In the preceding passage, Jesus says we should be standing by the door fully dressed, expecting the master of the house to return at any moment. For us this would mean we are "wearing" our baptismal commitment, for we are engaged in living out our faith. Here Peter asks if the example is for the disciples or for everyone in general. Immediately Jesus directs his call for preparedness toward the disciples. Any observant and diligent servant, he says, would go about his duties with equal diligence whether his master was in the house or on his way home. As the future leaders of God's people, the disciples had to be prudent and prepared because others would rely on them for direction. They were to be the first responders of the kingdom. Jesus promises that when the master finds everything running smoothly, he will reward the faithful servant with even more responsibility.

What does this say to us? That more will be expected isn't necessarily welcome news for someone who feels burdened trying to live the life of a faithful Christian. Our life with Christ requires a lot of diligence and vigilance. Will we be up to taking on more? Yes, because the master puts on his apron and waits on the servant whom he finds prepared. He will give what is needed of grace and strength for the requests he makes of us. If we are prepared we will be able to see this and rejoice.

Oratio

Dear Jesus, Master of my house, teach me to be alert to your presence, always ready for your arrival. Teach me to be a faithful steward of your gifts, alert and kind toward the others serving with me. I do not know the day of your final coming, but the kingdom is also here and now. Keep me ready to serve, ready to witness, ready to rejoice with you at every moment and for all eternity. Amen.

Contemplatio

Lord, I am alert to your coming.

Thursday of the Twenty-Ninth Week of Ordinary Time

∴·············∴

Lectio

Luke 12:49–53

Meditatio

> *"There is a baptism with which I must be baptized . . ."*

Although commentaries disagree about whether Jesus' "baptism" means his death or Pentecost, the reference to Jesus' *reception* of this baptism suggests the former. In that case, a literal translation could be: "A catastrophe is going to overwhelm me, and how I dread it, until it's over!"

I think we can picture Jesus feeling like that. After all, he was fully human, except that he never sinned. I can ask myself: Wouldn't I feel dread if I knew I'd undergo a violent death a few weeks or months from now? I wonder which would be worse—to know the day, hour, and details, or not to know them? Whichever would be worse, I suspect that was what Jesus experienced. To put it another way, his passion probably lasted much longer than twenty hours.

To me, the *baptism* is the key to the rest of the passage. In light of Jesus' death, the *fire*—although it could refer to God's judgment—seems to mean the descent of the Spirit. Jesus was eager that the Spirit come, but he had to pass through his "baptism" first. Then the Spirit could be sent. The divided households would result from people's acceptance or rejection of Jesus' identity and mission. Jesus' sufferings would have been increased by the knowledge that not everyone would accept the salvation he wanted to bring.

Oratio

Jesus, the dread you felt must have almost overpowered you, yet you kept on going. When I realize how anxious I get over the smallest things, I feel ashamed. Don't I believe that you will see me through my little difficulties? You always have before. I want to be more grateful to you for everything you've done, and to show this gratitude by living as a true Catholic in a divided world. My family members, friends, and coworkers might go in different directions, and while I want to be good to them in every way possible, I also intend to remain faithful to what I believe. Please give me the balance I need to walk this tightrope.

Contemplatio

Cast your fire into my heart, O Lord.

Friday of the Twenty-Ninth Week
of Ordinary Time

∴ · · · · · · · · · · · · ∴

Lectio

Luke 12:54–59

Meditatio

" . . . why do you not know how to interpret the present time?"

I think most of us can relate to what Jesus is saying. It is fairly easy to notice the differences in nature and interpret them to know what the weather will be like. Not only is weather easy to observe, it's also a safe topic. It's interesting that weather comes up frequently in friendly conversations. Human nature hasn't changed all that much in two thousand years. What would it take to interpret the present time? A discerning heart and the ability to see the bigger picture outside of ourselves.

Perhaps an example taken from another part of the Bible will help. Those who wrote the Pentateuch wanted to convey that God was actively involved in the lives of the patriarchs. This awareness allowed God to reveal himself to them in amazing ways. Because they lived with this awareness, figures like Abraham, Isaac, Jacob, and Joseph could interpret their "present time" in a discerning way, aware of God's call through the events of their daily lives. Joseph, in particular, stands out for me. What more painful circumstance can anyone face than being sold into slavery by his own brothers? Yet Joseph discerns the larger picture—a picture that includes God's plan. "God, therefore, sent me on ahead of you to ensure for you a remnant on earth and to save your lives in an extraordinary deliverance. So it was not really you but God who had me come here" (Gn 45:7–8).

Unfortunately, many contemporaries of Jesus failed to realize how God was present among them in his Son. We, too, can fail to recognize God's immediate presence with us. Discernment, then, means allowing God to reveal to us how he is working through our lives and the lives of others to affect the flow of human events.

Oratio

Jesus, like those to whom you spoke, I miss the meaning of a lot that happens in my life. I find it difficult to understand the events in my life and in the world in a way that allows you to communicate their meaning. So I can miss your presence in my life and in the world. May your Holy Spirit inspire me so the next time I wonder why something is happening, I might turn to you to help me understand. Let this become the way that I am habitually aware of what happens around me so that your plan may be accomplished through me. Amen.

Contemplatio

Lord, may I see in order to interpret the present time.

Saturday of the Twenty-Ninth Week of Ordinary Time

∴ · · · · · · · · · · · · ∴

Lectio

Luke 13:1–9

Meditatio

> *" . . . leave it for this year also. . . ."*

On April 30, 2000, Pope John Paul II canonized Faustina Kowalska (1905–1938). Saint Faustina lived an obscure life in her Polish convent, hidden from the eyes of the world. Yet through this humble sister, God gave the world a message of divine mercy—a message that the world needs now more than ever.

In a way, Faustina's life parallels what Jesus is saying in this parable. He's telling us to look beneath appearances. To the hasty observer, it might have seemed that the people who were killed by Pilate and by the falling tower in Siloam had been cursed by God. And the barren fig tree was obviously a lost cause, just some deadwood cluttering up the ground. Why not get rid of it? But Jesus says no, those unfortunate people were no more guilty than anyone else. And God, the Master Gardener, sees the potential of the seemingly lifeless tree. He wants to pour out more fertilizer on it, to coax it to bear fruit. And just as with the tree, God pours out ever more graces even on the most hopeless soul, the one who seems least likely to profit from it. Has that young man gotten caught up in a world of drugs, violence, and crime? Has that young woman already had an abortion and lost her sense of direction in life? God still pours out graces on them, cultivating the soil of their souls, fertilizing them like gentle rain, calling them back to his loving heart. The message of divine mercy is already in the Gospel. Yet Jesus chose to use Saint Faustina as an instrument to help people hear it in a new way. That is the beauty of the saints in the Church. Each of them lives an aspect of the Gospel in a startlingly new way, one that makes it fresh and alive for each new generation.

Oratio

Jesus, I trust in your merciful love. You know how often I have failed in the past, yet you keep on offering me mercy and forgiveness. Thank you, Lord, for your infinite patience with me. Help me to have complete confidence in your love.

Contemplatio

"Turn away your face from my sins; blot out all my guilt" (Ps 51:11).

Thirtieth Sunday of Ordinary Time—
Year A

⁙

Lectio

Matthew 22:34–40

Meditatio

> " . . . *with all your mind*."

How do you love with your mind? The founder of my religious congregation, Blessed James Alberione, often wrote that the mind is key. Confronted now with this sentence from the Gospel, I reviewed some of what Blessed James taught. He used the terms mind, will, heart, and body to refer to the whole person. Clearly Jesus means the whole person when he speaks of heart, soul, and mind or understanding (as well as strength, which is found in related passages).

Choices and actions follow thoughts. So do emotions, which influence choices. This situates *mind* at the root of most of our activity. So loving God with our mind would mean cultivating thoughts that please the Lord, never thoughts that could lead to sin. In fact, as we recall, one way that Jesus made the commandments more complete was by teaching that thoughts themselves can be sinful. On the positive side, we can grow in love of God by using our minds to seek deeper understanding of everything related to him.

Growth in knowledge of God should bring about deeper love for God.

And then there's the second Great Commandment, love of neighbor. It's not surprising that love of neighbor also involves our mind. For example, to love in the Gospel sense is to "wish well"—to will the other's good—and act accordingly. It's hard to wish someone well if we harbor unkind judgments about that person and his or her actions. It's easier to wish well if we think well. And emotions follow thoughts, thereby reinforcing our wishing the other well. Now, I ask myself: What does all this mean for me? What kinds of thoughts do I need to curb or redirect?

Oratio

Holy Spirit, Giver of wisdom, understanding, and counsel, enlighten me. I recognize that my emotions and choices are fed by my thoughts. Help me to be more aware of them. Sometimes my feelings may alert me to thoughts that need curbing or redirecting. Guide me in discovering these. I want to love totally the Father, the Son and you, Holy Spirit, and to love my neighbors as you love them.

Contemplatio

The mind is key.

Thirtieth Sunday of Ordinary Time—
Year B

⁝· · · · · · · · · · · · ·⁝

Lectio

Mark 10:46–52

Meditatio

> " . . . *many rebuked him, telling him to be silent.*
> *But he kept calling out all the more. . . .*"

Today's Gospel has no red tape, no official procedures, no process to get things done. It's plain and simple. Bartimaeus feels the fire of Jesus' presence and sees possibilities for a new life. He begins to cry out, and he isn't going to let the others in the crowd squelch that dream. Perhaps all the people following Jesus, maybe even the apostles themselves, are lazily listening, trailing behind the Master, soaking in what he says. Bartimaeus, however, wants action. He seizes the moment and takes Jesus at his word. Lord, I want to see!

Where are you? Is your discipleship lazily moving along? Does it involve Mass on an occasional Sunday, extra donations here and there, Christmas and Easter celebrated in style, token comments on debates over issues that touch on morality? Or do you have a Bartimaeus type of discipleship? Do you go straight to Jesus? Do you tell him what you need, what you want? Do you know what you want, what you most deeply want? Do you have a vision for your life as a

Christian? Are you growing, changing, maturing? Do you set goals? Do you have groups or companions for accountability? Do you live your relationship with Jesus as the most vital part of your life?

Jesus can make you aware, if you want to be. He can take away your blindness, deafness, confusion, and illusions. He can make your heart soft and compassionate. He can reinstate you in the community. He will do whatever it takes to bind you to him. Don't just follow the crowd. Don't just talk about Jesus and his agreeable sayings. Don't just argue over newspaper headlines about the Catholic Church. Be a Bartimaeus Christian and get something done in your life. What do you really want? Take some time to reflect on that question because when you go to Jesus, he will ask you, "What do you want me to do for you?"

Oratio

Lord, heal my blindness, that I may see you wherever you are. You are in the tabernacle in the Church. You are also in the eyes of a tiny child asking for help, or in the calloused hand of a homeless person begging for a handout. You are in a spouse, in a mother or father, in a colleague at work, in students in a classroom, in doctors in the hospital. Lord, I want to see you wherever you are.

Contemplatio

What do I really want?

Thirtieth Sunday of Ordinary Time—
Year C

⁝·············⁝

Lectio

Luke 18:9–14

Meditatio

> *"O God, be merciful to me a sinner."*

I like this story in Luke. I should, for by now I have lived it a million times! One of my friends will often remind me, "It's *not* about you. It's about *him*." Jesus addresses this parable to "those who were convinced of their own righteousness and despised everyone else." I understand righteousness to mean being in right relationship, in harmony, with God, neighbor, and self. How can you be in right relationship with God or anybody else if you despise anyone?

So what is going on in this story? Jesus wants us to know how to pray, and gives us two types of behavior: one to avoid, one to emulate. The attitude to avoid is one in which the Pharisee thanks God for himself and his own excellence. Being biased in his own favor, he compares himself to his neighbor, who comes up short. The tax collector, instead, doesn't look around, doesn't compare himself, doesn't offer accomplishments or excuses. He just presents himself to the Author of Life and says, "O God, be merciful to me a sinner." In this parable, the Lord teaches us that humility is key. Why? Because he wants more for us. To receive it, we need to come out of our smug little worlds where each of us reigns supreme. The Lord wants to gift us with the fullness of his life and kingdom. He tells us, "Everything I have is yours" (Lk 15:31). In order to enjoy this "everything," we need to let go of always needing to be right and to measure everything by our own criteria. Rather, it's all about God. It's all about letting God be God, keeping our eyes on his goodness and asking for his help. We need to keep our places, as people belonging to him, adopted in Christ. In the truth of who we are, we can ask humbly and confidently, "be merciful to me a sinner." One cannot earn this gift; it is freely given with love.

Oratio

Dear God, sometimes I don't trust you enough because of my fear. I know I fail, but I'd rather point out other people's faults than admit to my own. You are our Father, who loves us all and desires our good. Teach me to let go of judging others, since I lack your divine wisdom, mercy, and love. Help me keep my eyes on you and your mercy, trusting that you will forgive and heal all of us. Help me be grateful for the person you have made me, and the gift I can offer you of a loving, humble heart.

Contemplatio

Lord, it's all about you. I am so grateful for your gifts.

Monday of the Thirtieth Week
of Ordinary Time

⁚· · · · · · · · · · · ·⁚

Lectio

Luke 13:10–17

Meditatio

> " . . . *you are set free.* . . ."

Today's Gospel tells about a spontaneous healing miracle that takes place on the Sabbath. Usually, when Jesus healed someone, he asked for some sort of manifestation of faith—not just any faith, but the kind that moves mountains. Today's Gospel of a miracle on the Sabbath has none of that. It seems as though Jesus simply turns his attention toward a long-suffering woman and tells her, "Woman, you are set free of your infirmity."

Pointedly ignoring Jesus, the local official then chides the crowds for seeking healing on the Lord's day, telling them to come back during the work week. That's a hint that the crippled woman didn't just "happen" to be there: she has come for a healing. In other words, she has the faith that moves mountains, even if she doesn't verbally say, "Lord, I believe."

For his part, Jesus seems to have been deliberately provocative, working this miracle on the Sabbath, when all work is forbidden. After the official's reproof, Jesus even gives a bit of a homily. He explains that just as every one of the worshipers there that day would feed and water the farm animals on the Sabbath, there is no reason to deny life and health to human beings in their suffering. Even more, the Sabbath was made for just that purpose! It is a day of freedom for household servants, slaves, and even animals. No wonder Jesus doesn't use the language of a cure, but of freedom: "You are set free."

Oratio

How much I need the freedom of Sabbath days and moments, Lord! These are the sacred times in which we who were made in your image and likeness rest from our labors, put aside the pressing and real commitments that wear us down, and meet you to receive your peace. Restore me here and now in the place that most needs your presence. Receive my burden, and exchange it for your yoke, which is easy, and your burden, which is light because you share it with me. That communion with you is my Sabbath rest.

Contemplatio

"For freedom Christ set us free" (Gal 5:1).

Tuesday of the Thirtieth Week
of Ordinary Time

❖·············❖

Lectio

Luke 13:18–21

Meditatio

"... *mustard seed* ... *yeast*...."

When I think of God, adjectives like almighty, strong, awe-inspiring, and magnificent spring to mind. In John's Gospel, Jesus tells his disciples that he is going to prepare a place for them (referred to as dwelling place or mansion) in his Father's house, in his Father's kingdom (see Jn 14:1–4). Growing up in a cramped apartment, I often dreamed about the great mansion in which I would one day live. So much in Scripture speaks about God's grandeur that it seems contradictory to describe the kingdom of God in terms of tiny mustard seeds and yeast as in today's Gospel.

With these images, Jesus speaks of small things that will become great or will have great effects. We are also reminded that God is found not just in the big things in life, but in the small ones as well. While we can stand in awe at the sight of a majestic tree, that tree began as a seed that grew into a little sapling. Small events or things can lead to greater ones, like a pebble thrown into a pond that causes ever-widening ripples.

Just so, a small act of love and kindness, which is a clue to the presence of God's kingdom, can lead to more acts of loving kindness or more signs of God's kingdom.

Several times I have had the awesome experience of seeing Niagara Falls. The sight is always beautiful and powerful. This natural wonder can remind us of our great God. But God is also present in small, everyday things. God is present in the wave a child gives as you pass by, or the cup of coffee a friend happens to bring you. These small gestures make us smile and brighten our day. They can help us act with loving kindness toward others, thus making God's kingdom more present.

Oratio

Open my eyes, Lord, that I may see your presence in everything around me, both the great and the small. Besides seeing your presence, your kingdom, around me, may I also be an active participant in this kingdom. Like the mustard seed and the handful of yeast, I too want to be a sign of your presence in our world, slowly witnessing to your love. You ask not for great acts, but that I do all things with love and kindness, thus making your kingdom more visible on this earth. Give me the grace to do so. Amen.

Contemplatio

Open my eyes, Lord!

Wednesday of the Thirtieth Week of Ordinary Time

∴ · · · · · · · · · · · · ∴

Lectio

Luke 13:22–30

Meditatio

"Strive to enter through the narrow gate. . . ."

Jesus is on his way to his destiny, to Jerusalem, and he is teaching as he goes along. Someone asks how many people will be saved. In his characteristic way, Jesus uses the question to teach about how to live. It is difficult to lift Jesus' words out of context and present them as his teachings—even John says that the world could not hold the books that could be written about Jesus' teachings (see Jn 21:25). Luke gives us gleanings that have withstood the test of time, and are clear enough for us to get the message. And what a message it is! Jesus reminds us that salvation, or acceptance into the kingdom, is not an easy affair. It will not be enough to say on the day of salvation, "We heard your teachings with our own ears," if we did not embrace those teachings. Jesus asks us not to squander the time of mercy, because the time of salvation will come for each person who walks this earth. It definitely requires our response and our commitment.

This message is about our need to be attentive and use the faculties, gifts, and graces God has provided for us, so that we will make our own personal response to Jesus' invitation, "Yes, Lord, I believe," and then live accordingly. This message is about the lengths to which God has gone in sending us his Son, the Life and Love who offered himself in sacrifice to redeem us all, even to death on the cross. This message is about how we can go ahead with trust and joy on the road to the kingdom, because Jesus, who walks before us, said, "I am the way" (Jn 14:6), and he has really experienced, as one of us, the trials and difficulties of that long road.

Oratio

Jesus, when I realize that you want to walk by my side, the road to the kingdom does not seem so narrow and rough. I want to receive each day as a gift, accepting it on my journey for what it is and what it helps me experience: loving others in you, and finding the wisdom that life lived in your presence will grow in me. But above all, I ask you to give me your own loving attentiveness toward the others with me on this journey, so that I will help to make it a journey of joy.

Contemplatio

Lord, walk with me.

Thursday of the Thirtieth Week of Ordinary Time

⋮ ⋅⋅⋅⋅⋅⋅⋅⋅⋅⋅⋅⋅ ⋮

Lectio

Luke 13:31–35

Meditatio

"Jerusalem, Jerusalem. . . ."

It seems that the meaning of "fox" hasn't changed much from New Testament times. For the people of the eastern Mediterranean basin, a fox was someone sly, malicious, and weak. In replying to Herod through the tetrarch's apparent emissaries, Jesus states that since prophets are killed only in Jerusalem, he will continue to go about freely while still in Herod's domain. And then comes that stirring lament: "Jerusalem, Jerusalem . . . how many times I yearned to gather your children together as a hen gathers her brood. . . ."

But who is speaking here? Luke hasn't related any incidents of Jesus' public life that took place in Jerusalem. I recall that line in John: "Whoever has seen me has seen the Father (Jn 14:9). The heart of the Son throbs in unison with the heart of the Father! This Father yearns for his children but has been rejected in the person of his prophets.

Throughout the Scriptures, the mystery of human freedom appears like a refrain. God wanted us to resemble him, so he gave us the ability to know, to love—and to choose. We often choose wrongly. Yet God never goes back on his commitment to humanity. He could wipe us out in an instant, but instead he rescues us again and again. So in today's reading we see the Son, who became human for our sake, weeping over Jerusalem, where he will give his very life for us.

Oratio

Father, Son, and Holy Spirit, have my words, actions, or attitudes caused you to weep over me? It's so easy to be thoughtless, to be heedless! Help me to sharpen my perceptions, make reflective judgments, and choose wisely. I want to use my freedom the way you intended—in imitation of you, Jesus, who always chose the good. Give me an enlightened and sensitive conscience. Help me to always approach the sacrament of Reconciliation with a new heart, ready to make a fresh beginning. And if the occasion arises, teach me how to lead others back to you.

Contemplatio

A new heart, a new start.

Friday of the Thirtieth Week
of Ordinary Time

❖ · · · · · · · · · · · · ❖

Lectio

Luke 14:1–6

Meditatio

> " . . . *on the Sabbath. . . .*"

Oh, that thorny Sabbath! It seems that every time Jesus turns around he is locking horns with someone over this day of rest. Today a man appears, suffering the joint pain and fever of edema, and everybody else wrangles over what's "lawful." Since Jesus is sharing a meal with lawyers of the Torah, whose giftedness lies in their razor-sharp minds, Jesus shrewdly frames his question to them in legal terms. Then, typically, he takes everyone a step further, from a father's—and his Father's—perspective, effortlessly healing the man in the process. They're dumbfounded. Apparently they forgot who heals. If God heals—they suppose that this Jesus has no curative power of his own—then God must want to make his loved ones whole even on the Sabbath, *especially* on the Sabbath. With his example, Jesus challenges them to examine what this rest is really for.

They know that it hearkens back to Genesis, when God rested from creating the world. God wasn't saying, "Finally we're done!" God's rest was not, as some imagine, divine inactivity. Look around: creation continues, even on *Shabbat*. God is pictured rejoicing at all that's been accomplished and at how very good it is (see Gn 1:31). Through it, God, Israel's bridegroom, reveals his love to his bride. How could Jesus not honor this rest and make this loved one whole? The Sabbath foreshadows that day when Jesus will share with us the ultimate rest he himself entered into with his risen humanity. ". . . a sabbath rest still remains for the people of God" (Heb 4:9). In Christian tradition, observance of Friday is meant to prepare us for the observance of Sunday. Why not begin anew with this Friday? How different our world would be if we paid more attention to this rhythm, two days in tandem, lived in tandem with the restorative life of God. This is the obedience of faith that is a condition for entering into God's rest (Heb 4:1ff.).

Oratio

"Lord even of the Sabbath," I could use a reality check. How often Sundays have been the day I can either get my personal or family chores and shopping done, or pursue my interests without thinking of yours. What am I doing to my life? To others' lives? To society? Besides my need for a little rest and recreation, I need time to focus the lens of my life on you. Help me find my happiness in looking to your glory—and that's *me, us,* fully alive, alive in you.

Contemplatio

May I rest in you.

Saturday of the Thirtieth Week of Ordinary Time

∴ · · · · · · · · · · · · ∴

Lectio

Luke 14:1, 7–11

Meditatio

> *"On a sabbath Jesus went to dine at the home*
> *of the one of the leading Pharisees. . . ."*

Jesus, why do you eat at the house of a Pharisee? What are you thinking? You have denounced the hypocrisy of the Pharisees and reproached the scribes and lawyers. They have been setting traps for you, hoping to get rid of you. They are clearly set against you. Why do you go to the house of a Pharisee to share the intimacy of a meal? I can't fathom it. How do you act there? Did you plan what to say? Did you think of some great remarks that would outwit your host? Did you come up with backhanded complements or sarcastic remarks that would beat them at their own game? Why did you walk into the hornet's nest? They are observing you. How can you eat under that scrutiny?

I can't understand, Jesus, because I wouldn't have been able to do it. There are some people I don't like—family members who don't talk to me, colleagues I don't get along with, difficult neighbors. I couldn't just sit down to eat with them. I would feel such anger in my heart. My mind would be racing with things I would like to say to them. I would be rehearsing how to tell them off or defend myself. I would be stilted, uneasy, and maybe even unpleasant. I try to steer clear of anyone who upsets me. Some days just thinking of them gets my blood boiling. How do you do it? It seems so natural: you go to dine at the home of one of the Pharisees.

I understand: Love is the answer. Even though they seek your life and make your life difficult, you love them. You have nothing to hide. You seek their well-being. You promote the possibility of their growth. You give them every chance possible to hear, to listen, to trust, to obey. Your word convicts me, Lord.

Oratio

Jesus, this moment is decisive for the rest of my life. Today I begin to love my enemies, to love those I disagree with or who disagree with me. I start to love those who offend me or whom I don't like. I will begin today to love the colleagues I don't get along with and those who refuse to talk to me. I love those who report me and make my life miserable. And one day may I have the grace and the joy of sitting down with each of these persons at the eternal feast laid out in heaven for your children. Amen.

Contemplatio

Today I gaze on the mystery of the way you loved.

Thirty-First Sunday of Ordinary Time—
Year A

⁝· · · · · · · · · · · ·⁝

Lectio

Matthew 23:1–12

Meditatio

> *" . . . you have but one master . . ."*

Jesus is the only person whom we can follow both in word and example. Unlike ours, Jesus' words and actions harmonize completely. So much continuity exists between them that in the Catholic tradition, both are considered to impart divine revelation. As the Son of God, Jesus is the image of the Father. Since Jesus' words and actions flow from the truth of his being, both reveal the Person of God the Father. This is why we are to choose Christ alone as our Master. The choice is not so much to imitate Christ as to make his life our own. In the fullest sense of the master/disciple, master/ apprentice relationship, imitation alone is not the intended result. Rather, the master imparts the whole of his life and expertise to the apprentice/disciple so that the unique art or craft acquired will endure even after his death.

That is what the Christian life is meant to be: that we replicate the Master's life so completely in our own that his saving life endures through us. It requires a connection or bond so intimate and unique that no other relationship on earth can eclipse it or be compared to it. So often we are attracted to the same types of behavior the Pharisees were prone to. Yet how empty that makes us feel. The emptiness modeled by Jesus, however, allowed him to disguise divinity in our nature so that, as a servant, he could save that nature from its emptiness. Should we choose Christ as our Master, his demands may seem "hard to carry" according to the world's standards. However, unlike the Pharisees, who offered no assistance to others, Jesus does help us. He gave his life so that we might have the supernatural life of grace necessary to live as he invites us to live. What greater attraction can there be to give over my life to anyone but Christ?

Oratio

Jesus, I have often compared others' behavior with my own, as if I were the paradigm of perfection to which others should aspire. I call myself Christian, yet it seems that I have made myself the "master"—something that you clearly told your disciples to avoid. I don't like being humbled, but that is necessary if I am to truly be your disciple. Teach me what true humility is, so my words and actions may be worthy of the name Christian. Amen.

Contemplatio

Jesus, you, and you alone, are my Master.

Thirty-First Sunday of Ordinary Time— Year B

∴· · · · · · · · · · · · ·∴

Lectio

Mark 12:28b–34

Meditatio

> *"Well said, teacher."*

Mark's Gospel—generally considered the first to be written—has a very human quality. Often we seem to be viewing events through the eyes of an actual witness: Jesus sleeping in a boat with his head *on a cushion*, looking *lovingly* at the rich young man, or gazing about *in anger*. Some early Christian writers thought that Mark wrote down what Peter preached, which would certainly account for the eyewitness quality of Mark's writing. Mark, Matthew, and Luke all relate a discussion about the Great Commandment that took place between Jesus and a scribe. But there are surprising differences in the three accounts. (Well, perhaps not so surprising, if we remember that a few decades had passed between the event and the writing.) Of course, the possibility exists that two or three scribes questioned Jesus at different times regarding the same all-important point. But commentators on the Scriptures consider this unlikely.

Matthew and Luke convey a negative impression of the scribe. He asks his question to "test" Jesus. Mark, instead, presents the scribe as a man who has deeply studied the Law and drawn his own conclusions. He sincerely wants to know whether Jesus' thoughts on the Great Commandment match his own. He and the Master quickly find themselves on the same wavelength. It's interesting that the scribe makes explicit what Jesus has implied, by adding, ". . . there is no other than he." It's as if this man had been mulling over these truths for years. I'm struck by his final comment: ". . . worth more than all burnt offerings and sacrifices," which Jesus affirms.

In reflecting on this double commandment and its practice today, I get the impression that the pendulum may have swung too far *toward* good deeds and *away from* ritual. For many people, religion seems to consist in only helping others and not worshiping God. Instead, we're called to do both, as the two parts of the Great Commandment indicate.

Oratio

Jesus, Divine Master, I ask to understand the Great Commandment correctly, not neglecting either aspect. You commended the scribe for his wisdom. Help me to acquire his kind of wisdom and to balance my responsibilities to my sisters and brothers with my duties toward you. Amen.

Contemplatio

"There is no other commandment greater than these."

Thirty-First Sunday of Ordinary Time—
Year C

⁘ · · · · · · · · · · · · ⁘

Lectio

Luke 19:1–10

Meditatio

> " . . . *Zacchaeus . . . was seeking to see who Jesus was.* . . ."

Jesus is passing through the town of Jericho, accompanied by his disciples and a curious, admiring crowd. Zacchaeus is part of that curious crowd, anxious to get a look at the Master. Jesus does not intend to stay at anyone's house in Jericho, but is only passing through. Zacchaeus doesn't seem interested in becoming a follower of Jesus. He just wants to see this Jesus that everyone is talking about. Zacchaeus is curious, so he runs ahead and climbs a tree on the side of the road where Jesus will pass.

Now he can see Jesus coming up the road. As the crowd passes by, Jesus, moved by the Spirit, stops and looks up at Zacchaeus. Their eyes meet as Jesus gazes at the tax collector with a look of profound love that penetrates Zacchaeus' heart. Then, beyond his wildest imagination, Zacchaeus hears Jesus call him by name. Jesus wants to stay at *his* house today. Zacchaeus is beside himself with joy—he, a despised tax collector, a sinner—is to have the Master as his guest! He scrambles down from his perch on the tree. Critics in the crowd voice their displeasure at Jesus for choosing to go to the house of a sinner. But Zacchaeus has already been transformed by this encounter with Jesus. He sees Jesus as the Lord who loves him and extends his mercy toward him. Zacchaeus had amassed a great deal of wealth, sometimes deviously. But now all that is going to change. He tells the Lord he will make restitution, and Jesus praises his faith and repentance in the presence of witnesses. Jesus has found a lost lamb; salvation has come to Zacchaeus' house—all because Zacchaeus wanted to see Jesus, and Jesus looked up at him.

Oratio

Lord, like Zacchaeus, I too want to see you, to know you more and more. Often I cannot see you because my concerns, anxieties, and sins block me from focusing on you. Help me today to see how I can rise above all these things that get in the way. I will take some quality time to pray. You gaze upon me and call me by name. You see my desire to experience your love and mercy. Come to my "house" and show me what I must do to be reconciled with you, and the poor and hurting around me. Today, I recommit myself to loving and serving you in a concrete way.

Contemplatio

Come, Lord Jesus! May we meet each other on the way.

Monday of the Thirty-First Week of Ordinary Time

⁘ · · · · · · · · · · · · ⁘

Lectio

Luke 14:12–14

Meditatio

" . . . do not invite your friends . . . they may invite you back . . ."

"Social etiquette according to Jesus" could be the subtitle for chapter 14 of Luke's Gospel. In the verses before this passage, Luke tells us that Jesus has accepted an invitation to dine at the house of a leading Pharisee. Jesus tells a story to his fellow guests when he notices how they are competing for better seats. In today's Gospel, Jesus evidently has been listening to his dining companions discuss their impending social obligation to reciprocate by inviting the host to their houses. Always full of surprises, Jesus addresses his host, saying clearly that the next time he throws a party he should not expect to be repaid. In other words, the intention with which we do things is as important as the actual deed.

Throughout the Gospels, especially in Luke, we see how Jesus upholds the dignity of all persons. In Jesus' remarks to his dinner host about whom to invite to his next party, he lists groups of people who may not be in the host's address book—the poor, the blind, and the lame.

Jesus warns the Pharisee, the dinner guests, and us about getting lost in the details of social expectations that may make us forget our real obligations. As members of the family of God, we are obliged to take care of our own. If we get too caught up in questions of status and position, we may overlook our basic obligations. Jesus reminds us that his Heavenly Father will repay our good deeds and intentions because nothing we do goes unnoticed.

Oratio

Father in heaven, I believe in your love for me. I want to be more aware of the beautiful things you do for me, so that I can share your goodness with others. I often start out with the right intention, but then my need for appreciation gets in the way. I hope that the good I am able to do for my sisters and brothers will truly reflect your love and concern for them. I ask this in the name of Jesus, who is my Life.

Contemplatio

Purify my heart.

Tuesday of the Thirty-First Week
of Ordinary Time

⁝ · · · · · · · · · · · · ⁝

Lectio

Luke 14:15–24

Meditatio

> " . . . *they all began to excuse themselves.*"

Once I heard in a homily or talk that invitations to great banquets like this one were extended weeks in advance, with the invited persons committing themselves right away. If that was the custom, it's no wonder that the wealthy man in Jesus' parable was disturbed when his intended guests didn't appear for the dinner. They certainly had advance notice! On the other hand, I later read that a precise date was not always set for such a feast. (This is supported by the servant being sent to say that the great dinner "is now ready.") Yet even from this perspective, some of those invited give lame excuses for their absence. And don't those excuses sound uncomfortably familiar? Don't they resemble our own excuses?

In reflecting on this parable, I started thinking about commitments. Too many commitments can box a person in. One can become tense and irritable, and perhaps fail to follow through, thereby souring relationships. It seems better, as I see it, to make fewer commitments and honor them than to make many promises and be quick to pull out. Jesus taught that someone who is trustworthy in small matters will also be trustworthy in greater ones (see Lk 16:10)—and our *major* commitments, of course, are very important. We don't want to fail in those.

To habitually look for an easy way out is to place oneself on a slippery slope. It's better to take the alternate route, even though the upward path will be rocky.

Athletes improve their skills through rigorous training.

Practice is the key to mastery.

A lifetime of fidelity consists of many small acts of faithfulness.

Oratio

Lord Jesus, I want to choose my commitments wisely and follow through on them—trying not to let other people down. May I remember that fidelity in small matters can strengthen my faithfulness to the major commitment (or commitments) to which you have called me. Please help me to avoid the slippery slope so that I may climb the rugged path, knowing that your grace will sustain me. I ask you to accompany me, step by step, so that I may persevere to the end. Amen.

Contemplatio

Follow through.

Wednesday of the Thirty-First Week of Ordinary Time

∴ · · · · · · · · · · · · ∴

Lectio

Luke 14:25–33

Meditatio

> *"In the same way, everyone of you*
> *who does not renounce all his possessions. . . ."*

"In the same way. . . ." That's a curious statement. Jesus just told two stories of people protecting things in their care: First, the man building a tower to protect a house or a vineyard; second, the king going to battle, which is usually done to protect one's country. Jesus says these persons sit down and calculate whether they can finish the job or not. Then he tells us that we must *renounce* our possessions—in the same way, with the same attentiveness, with the same energy. In this passage Jesus places three requirements on the great crowds following him. He says that to be his disciples, we must love him more than our family and even ourselves, we must carry our cross, and we must willingly give up or set aside *all* our possessions.

These are stiff requirements—or perhaps they are gifts. Jesus is clearly inviting us to take on his own attitudes and dispositions. He himself left the communion of the Trinity, emptied himself, and for love of us became a man and walked this earth. He loved us more than himself and his own life, when he willingly handed himself over to be crucified so that in his death we might be saved from sin and darkness. He embraced the cross so that we might discover that in our "passion," too, we will find the new life of glory welling up in our souls. Finally, Saint Paul tells us that Jesus did not cling to equality with God but poured himself out completely in becoming the son of Mary, totally dependent on her and Joseph. He traded the riches of heavenly glory for the lilies of the field and hard work in Joseph's carpentry shop. Following Jesus will stretch us and bend us and break us until selfishness is expunged from our hearts. Then what a gift it will be to live openly for others, and not to have to defend and protect ourselves, our ideas, our possessions. What a consolation when suffering will reveal to us the precious gold of transformation and new life, and its mysteries will be a source of peace.

Oratio

My heart lies open before you, my Lord and love. It is weak, so be careful with it. Its only strength is its desire to live a truly Christian life in every way. Take me at my word today and make me less selfish and more giving. Amen.

Contemplatio

Jesus, come.

Thursday of the Thirty-First Week of Ordinary Time

∴ · · · · · · · · · · · · ∴

Lectio

Luke 15:1–10

Meditatio

"Rejoice with me. . . ."

Chapter 15 of Luke's Gospel contains a triptych of parables with the theme of finding what is lost. Today's passage relates the first two parables—the lost sheep and the lost coin. Both parables contain the words, "rejoice with me" when the lost has been found. Extrapolating these parables to the sinner being found by God, a two-sided rejoicing occurs. First there is the joy of the finder and, second, the joy of the one found.

While praying with this Scripture passage I remembered times when I lost some*thing* (like my watch or cell phone), and how I searched until I found it. Then I recalled a time when I physically lost some*one*. When I was in high school I took my three-year-old brother with me to a local museum and I lost him. I searched everywhere I could think of but I could not find him. I was crying hysterically, thinking that someone might have kidnapped him. After searching for about fifteen minutes I went to tell our mother, who was waiting for us at the entrance, that her son was lost. On my way there, I over-heard a security guard ask, "What's your name, little boy?" I looked up and saw my brother! I was crying as I shouted his name and held him close to me. I was filled with such indescribable joy, and I knew instantly how much I loved him. I wanted to hold him forever and never let him go so he couldn't ever get lost or hurt again.

That is how God responds to us when we have gotten lost due to sin and come wandering back. He rejoices and holds us close. But he doesn't trap us, he lets us go off on our own, preserving our free will, ready to seek us out the next time we stray. What an exhilarating joy it is to know that God rejoices over us at all times!

Oratio

"Rejoice with me"—is that how you feel, Lord? Are you rejoicing that you have found me and called me back? You rejoice that you have found me in that dark cave of sin and brought me into your light. I rejoice that you always find me. I know you will not hold me tight forever; instead you place me gently by your side. For now, Lord, hold me in your arms. Remind me throughout this day that you rejoice, and I in turn will rejoice because you, my God, remain faithful and will not let me stay lost. Amen.

Contemplatio

I rejoice with you, Lord.

Friday of the Thirty-First Week of Ordinary Time

∴⋯⋯⋯∴

Lectio

Luke 16:1–8

Meditatio

> *"For the children of this world are more prudent in dealing
> with their own generation than the children of light."*

Jesus liked to use parables in his teaching because they were a way of involving his listeners. Parables allow us to make a judgment on a given situation, and then apply that lesson to our own lives. In this way we become radically involved and are real participants in the story. In today's parable Jesus commends the prudence and farsightedness of the steward. This wily man prepares for his future state of unemployment by reducing the bills of his master's debtors. In this way he assures himself that they will welcome him into their homes in the future.

Are we as concerned about our eternal future as this shrewd steward is for his temporal one? Or are we a bit complacent and at times even a little lazy? Jesus wants to drive home this central point of the parable. It's easy for us as Christians who practice our faith to answer with a comfortable "of course I'm preparing for my eternal future." But if we are honest, we have to admit that we sometimes put our spiritual life on the back burner.

The steward begins by taking concrete, decisive steps while he still has time. What am I doing now to secure my future in the next life? Do I take time for daily prayer and reflection on God's word? Do I offer my services to a neighbor in need when this is possible? Do I strive to grow in knowledge of my faith? If I am complacent, then I am fulfilling Jesus' statement that "the children of this world are more prudent in dealing with their own generation than are the children of light." Instead, let us learn from Jesus and make the concrete everyday choices that will lead us to our goal of eternal life.

Oratio

Jesus, time passes quickly and so does my life. Help me to use well the time and the gifts you have given me. Help me to be like the prudent and wise virgin who lived with her eyes fixed on her master's return. For then will I be well prepared and ready for life eternal.

Contemplatio

Come, Lord Jesus, come!

Saturday of the Thirty-First Week
of Ordinary Time

⋮⋯⋯⋯⋯⋮

Lectio

Luke 16:9–15

Meditatio

> *". . . God knows your hearts . . ."*

This Gospel is hard to comprehend. ". . . [M]ake friends for yourselves with dishonest wealth," Jesus says, "so that when it fails, you will be welcomed into eternal dwellings." Jesus seems to be preaching an anti-Gospel here. He appears to be praising the dishonest, the scheming, the thieves. This touches a tender wound in these days of mortgage scams, corporate bailouts, and loan schemes. How many individuals and organizations have been bilked out of their livelihoods by the very patterns Jesus seems to be recommending? But is this really what he is saying? This passage follows the story of the wily manager who knew the pink slip was coming because he had been caught in dishonesty. He immediately devises another plan to ensure that those whom he had helped in his dishonesty would take him in. His boss praises him "for acting prudently."

As Jesus tells this story, he is actually making a snide remark in order to get our attention. Be enterprising, he tells us. If we are going to go about life wasting the gifts God gives us, we had better have a plan because our wasteful ways will betray us. When the day of accounting arrives, whose hands will we have played into? The better plan is to be trustworthy in our use of every little grace of time, and then at death, God will gladly entrust us with the kingdom. We are servants in our dealings with God. The only choice is this: to be wily or willing. We cannot serve two masters, so we have to make a basic decision. The Gospel says it is between God and money, but we can safely say that it is between the ways of God and the ways of the world. We cannot pretend before God, for he reads our hearts.

Oratio

Dear Lord, you do know our hearts. You know we are weak and easily distracted from our duties by the cares, commitments, and curiosities of this life. We are impatient for the kingdom and begin to look for it in all the wrong places. We forget that we can make no pretension before you, and offer no alibis or excuses. We are an open book in your presence. Give us the ability to write a life of Good News so that we will be welcomed into the kingdom as good and faithful servants. Amen.

Contemplatio

Make me trustworthy in the little and the great things of life.

Thirty-Second Sunday of Ordinary Time— Year A

:·············:

Lectio

Matthew 25:1–13

Meditatio

" . . . [They] took their lamps and went out to meet the bridegroom."

What did these virgins do that was so important? They were there. *There.* They "went out to meet the bridegroom." They decided to do one simple thing—to be *present.* What does it mean to be present? To be so fully present that I genuinely listen with eyes, ears, mind, and heart? In an age that has surpassed all previous generations in the dubious art of multitasking, am I able to be present to the Lord? One of the first steps in prayer is so simple, yet so elusive. It is simply to be there, *present*— to show up, attentive and open, and simply *be* with the Lord.

Saint Teresa of Avila approached this parable like a lover. The bridegroom represents the Lord, and she was in love with the Lord. She sees the story of the virgins as a model for prayer, for those who love the Lord. Teresa reminds us that the gift of prayer comes only from God, yet we too have a part to play. Our part is to be present, to *be there.* When we purposely give the Lord our full attention by spending time exclusively with him, we are telling God that he means that much to us. What a precious gift we offer the Lord in an age in which time is at such a premium! To deliberately give the Lord time in prayer can be an act of faith, hope, and love. We *believe* God cares about us, so we go to meet him. Prayer is a gift, and God may choose to give us that gift today or not (we know not when the bridegroom may appear), but we go to meet God with the *hope* that God will make his presence known to us. To give the Lord such undivided attention, without demanding that he respond, is a genuine gift of *love*—a reciprocal gift of love, because the Lord will not be outdone in generosity.

Oratio

Lord, I want to be fully present to you when I pray, so help me to trust that you will provide for me in that prayer, just as I need it. Help me to trust that you will come to meet me. All I need to do is find those ways and moments to be present to you. And since you are always present in those around me, help me practice by being fully present to others in my daily encounters with them.

Contemplatio

You desire to meet me, Lord, so I want to be there to meet you.

Thirty-Second Sunday of Ordinary Time—
Year B

⁘ · · · · · · · · · · · · ⁘

Lectio

Mark 12:38–44

Meditatio

> " . . . all she had. . . ."

In the Gospel readings these past few Sundays, scribes have not fared well. Today Jesus castigates those who, in avarice and lust for prestige, twist the Law to line their own pockets, even at the expense of society's most vulnerable members—widows. In a different twist, one of those widows unwittingly bests both that crowd and the rich, whose offerings clatter in the treasury boxes that line the Temple walls. As if to sketch the face of true worship, Jesus observes that she "contributed all she had," not to extol giving that harms the giver, but to laud the offering of the heart.

Chances are, we've all been muscled into a donation of some kind. We may have wished that a lighter heart could have accompanied the lighter wallet. Our reluctance may stem less from selfishness than from caution. We want to give to a "worthy cause." We might even want to control how our contribution—money, time, energy, talent—is appropriated. That may be prudent; after all, in trying to do good with our limited resources we don't want to feel we're spinning our wheels. But such clinging can tarnish the Godlike sheen that comes from a spontaneous, lavish outpouring of love. Whether we give or receive, if we look only at the numbers, we miss the Gospel's point.

Do I resist giving of myself, including my prayer, because no one can guarantee its "success"? Do I compare myself with others and demur, with the excuse that my small contribution won't make a dent anyway? Our widow doesn't seem to care either way. What does it matter if others give more? She is free. It only matters that God esteems her gift of the heart. The Gospel story's paschal/liturgical dimension backlights another sacrificial love: the Crucified/Risen One himself and the Eucharist—one life, one loaf, one cup, emptied for the lives of many.

Oratio

Jesus, our poor widow couldn't have known that within a few decades the Temple she had supported would be a failed enterprise, not "one stone left upon another" (Mk 13:2). She gave without calculation or certainty, except for the belief that the God of Israel, her God, deserved all she had and was. May I give like that! In view of the good to be done, what I have, even all of it, seems like a pittance. But I know that's what you want. In your hands, it's more than just mine. It's ours; use it where it's needed most.

Contemplatio

Mary, widowed mother, thank you for giving us your Son—your *self*.

Thirty-Second Sunday of Ordinary Time— Year C

∴⋯⋯⋯∴

Lectio

Luke 20:27–38

Meditatio

> " . . . *he is not God of the dead,*
> *but of the living, for to him all are alive."*

In this passage, the Sadducees put an odd, complicated case to Jesus. Since the story is all about what will occur at the resurrection of the dead, which they deny, it is evident that the question is disingenuous. They are just trying to make the whole idea of the afterlife look ridiculous. In his response, Jesus refutes their idea that there will be no resurrection of the dead. How do we know that there is life beyond death? Because the God of Abraham, Isaac, and Jacob is not the God of the Dead (a repugnant name, his adversaries would agree), but the God of Life, of the living. To God, everyone is alive. It might seem that Abraham is long dead and gone, but God is eternal, and the immortal souls of all people are known to him and loved by him.

This is one of the most consoling truths of our faith. The people we have loved on earth, and who have died, have not ceased to exist. Our bodies eventually stop working and death comes, but our souls cannot die. And at the end of time, God will bring our souls and bodies back together again, and our resurrected bodies will never die. We have no idea what the experience of death and existence without our bodies will be like. We may look toward it with fear, resignation, or a sense of adventure, or we may simply try to avoid looking at it. But whatever our attitude may be, we know our God is a God of the living. He holds all people in his hands. All are alive to him. As we draw near the end of the liturgical year, the Church chooses Scripture passages that help us look at the reality of the end times and of death (which is the end of the world for each of us).

Oratio

Well, Jesus, it's that time of year again. The Church seems to save all the Gospel readings about death, judgment, and the end of the world for these weeks of November. I sometimes get so caught up in life that I forget that we are waiting for you to come again. Then we will be united with all who have gone before us. Eternal life in communion with you— that is my desire. Help me keep it as the goal of all I do.

Contemplatio

Come, Lord Jesus!

Monday of the Thirty-Second Week of Ordinary Time

⁘············⁘

Lectio

Luke 17:1–6

Meditatio

"Be on your guard!"

I think I have to take Jesus seriously. After all, who's to say, "He's not speaking to me"? I don't like to consider stumbling blocks, much less millstones, but maybe I do need to reflect a bit about freedom. When I'm away from the workplace, church, and my charitable rounds, I like to relax and "be myself." I like to be free. But that's where the stumbling block might appear. Is everything I do or say in my free time what I'd want others to observe and imitate—especially the young?

Scripture says that after God freed the Israelites from slavery, he gave them the Ten Commandments. History relates that after the American Revolution, the founding fathers established a government and made laws. Freedom isn't supposed to be lawlessness. True freedom has its limits, which are the rights of others. God's children, however young or old they may be, have a right to my good example.

At times, I may even need to refrain from what would normally be permissible because someone else considers it sinful. Saint Paul found himself in such a situation at least once. He told the Corinthians that some Christians believed it a sin to eat meat that had been sacrificed to idols. Paul himself knew it wasn't wrong because an idol is nothing. But he declared that he wouldn't touch that meat if he knew that others would be disturbed—especially if they might follow his example and disobey their conscience in the process. They had a right to his blameless behavior (see 1 Cor 8:1–13).

So, my right to relax and "be myself" is curtailed by others' rights to my good example.

Oratio

Jesus, help me to be careful. I want to remember that I'm surrounded by impressionable people—whether young or not-so-young. They may look to me as an example more often than I think. Help me to always reflect you—to radiate you. Don't let me do anything, even with the best of goodwill, that could lead someone to sin. Help me to be alert, sensitive, and thoughtful. Amen.

Contemplatio

If there's no stumbling block, there will be no millstone.

Tuesday of the Thirty-Second Week
of Ordinary Time

∴··············∴

Lectio

Luke 17:7–10

Meditatio

> ". . . we have done what we were obliged to do."

This Gospel passage may rub us the wrong way, perhaps because of the master/servant language, perhaps because we live in a culture clearly based on a reward system. However, it might help to look at it from the perspective of our relationship with God. If an employee has agreed to perform a certain job, the employer can expect the employee to fulfill that commitment. This makes sense. Unlike the master/slave relationship, however, the employee is paid for his or her work. But since we are made in the image of God, God can expect us to fulfill the reality of being God's child simply because it is our reality. This expectation is difficult for us to make sense of. Even more so, those of us who have taken on the commitment of living the Christian life have freely assented to living up to this expectation. Since we have fully assumed the obligation, then we can be expected to fulfill the duties associated with that obligation and act accordingly.

But for some reason, the idea that God has this prerogative rubs many people, including many Christians, the wrong way, especially when it touches us in the area of personal morality. The only antidote to this is love. Falling in love with God will allow me not only to take on my obligations as his child, but also to fulfill them without resentment or making excuses for myself when it's difficult. Love allows me to give of myself unreservedly without seeking payment or reward. For love itself is the reward.

Of course, this requires us to make a choice. The fundamental choice is to let God be God, and for us to accept the awesome responsibility of being his children. If this choice directs our lives, we will be lifted out of ourselves and satisfied simply in performing our obligation in being children of God.

Oratio

Jesus, your words challenge me at this moment. At times it is hard for me to admit that you are God and that I owe you adoration and obedience. Yet you invite me to this relationship with you; you do not force it on me. I believe that I am made in your image and that you ask me to commit myself to living in your image. I now recommit myself to living the Christian life in which I was baptized. Help me to fulfill my obligations as a Christian out of love for you and your Father. Amen.

Contemplatio

Father, I am your servant. Blessed is my obligation.

Wednesday of Thirty-Second Week
of Ordinary Time

⋮· · · · · · · · · · · ·⋮

Lectio

Luke 17:11–19

Meditatio

> *"As they were going they were cleansed."*

Perhaps the ten lepers are lucky enough to be in the right place at the right time. Or perhaps this is a marvelous example of God's provident design. As outcasts, the lepers linger near the city gates, where they can hear of the mighty deeds and wonders that Jesus works. United by their dreaded disease, this small band of Jews includes a Samaritan, who would not otherwise have been welcome in their circle. As Jesus draws near, they raise their voices, boldly begging for mercy. We can imagine the scene. Jesus' gaze falls on them and in a single moment he perceives the depth of their anguish and the shame of their social stigma. All this captivates the most merciful heart of the Master. How can he resist this heartfelt cry for both pardon and release from suffering?

Interestingly, Jesus does not reach out to heal and restore them immediately. Rather, he sends them on their way, telling them to go show themselves to the priests. "As they were going, they were cleansed." Perhaps we too might recognize this pattern of gradual healing in our own lives. Personal sorrow or inner hurts might slowly diminish as we become more focused on giving ourselves in love to others. The marvelous gift of integration can help us arrive at a place of serenity and self-acceptance, despite our limitations or failures. Relief and release may come very slowly and even be barely perceptible at times. Perhaps this most often happens "on the way" of life and not in one magnificent moment. That should make us grateful.

Not all the lepers return to give thanks. Rather than think harshly of "the other nine" we might instead marvel at the extent of the grateful one's insight. His eyes are opened and he sees that he has been cured. So he runs back to Jesus with gratitude and praise.

Oratio

Jesus, I don't always recognize your loving providence at work in my life. Give me patience in times of adversity, and grace to bear interior trials with faith. Help me to work together with others to overcome injustice and prejudice against those who are despised or forgotten. Keep my gaze fixed on your face even in the midst of my earthly concerns. Gradually heal me of anything that keeps me from being free to grow in love. Thank you, Jesus, for the gift of faith and for the mercy you have shown me. May I live with a grateful heart and gladly bear witness to you with my life.

Contemplatio

I am attentive to God's presence always at work in me.

Thursday of the Thirty-Second Week of Ordinary Time

∴ · · · · · · · · · · · · ∴

Lectio

Luke 17:20–25

Meditatio

> *"Do not go off, do not run in pursuit [of spectacular signs]."*

Luke would be right at home with us. Some people still want signs. Predicting the end of the world, they see all kinds of clues proving their point. Even if we aren't taken up into this "end of the world" frenzy, we too want signs in our way. Let's be honest—it's hard to believe. Jesus doesn't promise to give us signs. But he does guarantee one thing: suffering. He will suffer greatly, and so will his disciples. And it is precisely this suffering that prompts many of us to demand signs. "Prove to me that you love me by taking this suffering away!" "How can God love me if he let this happen to me?" "Why did God do this to me?" It is human to want spectacular proof before we will believe. The scoffers at the foot of the cross jeered at Jesus, saying he should come down from the cross and save himself to prove his claim to be the Christ of God, the Chosen One. "Come off that cross and then we will believe," they challenged him. But Jesus did not comply with their demand.

We waste so much time by demanding that God prove himself to us before we believe. All spiritual development, however, pivots on the leap of faith into the abyss of the unknown and the incomprehensible, in the face of the mystery of suffering. And suffering comes into the lives of all of us. The lesson of today's Gospel is that we need to jump into the inexplicable events of our life in utter faith, and then we will discover that the one we have trusted is indeed faithful. It doesn't work the other way around. God cannot be bought. Just as the cross precedes the resurrection, the imprisonment of the apostles and the persecution of the Church precedes its expansion around the globe. I can tell you from my experience that this is infallibly true. God is absolutely faithful, and he absolutely demands faith.

Oratio

Jesus, even you wanted to escape the cross when, in the Garden of Olives, you asked your Father to remove the cup of suffering. I feel that you understand my fears, but I so long to live beyond them. I desire my heart to expand with the discovery of your love and fidelity beyond any dream of mine! All you saints of God, pray for me, that I may be brought to taste the splendid truth of God's love in the way that you have. Amen.

Contemplatio

All you saints of God, open to me the door to holiness.

Friday of the Thirty-Second Week of Ordinary Time

:⋯⋯⋯•:

Lectio

Luke 17:26–37

Meditatio

"Where, Lord?"

In reading this Gospel, we are impressed by all the horrible things recounted. Jesus speaks of the flood in Noah's time, the destruction of Sodom and Gomorrah in Lot's time, and the happenings at the end of the world. Some people will be snatched up with the Lord, while others will be left behind. His hearers then, and we now, want to know one thing, "Where, Lord?" We might also ask, "Why, Lord?" Why will one person be chosen and another left? Why does this random selection seem to happen in disasters, accidents, and sickness? Why are some injured and others killed while others walk away without a scratch?

Jesus doesn't answer our question. Perhaps there is no answer to why some suffer and others are spared. But on rereading this passage, we realize that Jesus is speaking of something larger than suffering and death. He is commenting on the coming of the reign of God. In the preceding verses Jesus has made it clear that this reign is already here. God's reign has begun in Jesus himself. First, however, Jesus tells them he must suffer. And while this great work of God is taking place, life around him continues normally, just as it did before the flood. People are eating, drinking, and marrying, unaware of what is taking place in their midst. The same thing happened in Lot's time. People went about buying and selling, building and planting. And so it will be even as the Son of Man is manifested in the current day, says Jesus. Here Jesus could be drawing a picture of the end times or merely stating the obvious: that some people will leave everything to follow him. "One will be taken, the other left." The people listening to him ask, "Where, Lord?" Jesus replies with an odd image. "Where the body is," he says, "there also the vultures will gather." In other words, the coming of God's reign will be obvious and undeniable, just as when we see vultures swarming, we know something is dead.

Oratio

Lord, open our eyes to your kingdom. Help us to discern you working in daily life and in the great events that surround us. Let us be prepared for every indication of your coming. Keep our faith in you lively and our hearts engaged in loving you. May we always freely question you so that you can direct us as you will. "When, Lord?" "Where, Lord?" "Why, Lord?" These questions are music to your ears, Lord. These are the cries, the prayers, the songs that crescendo in the great *alleluia* of your heavenly reign. May it be so.

Contemplatio

"So it will be on the day the Son of Man is revealed."

Saturday of the Thirty-Second Week of Ordinary Time

⁘ · · · · · · · · · · · · ⁘

Lectio

Luke 18:1–8

Meditatio

> " . . . *justice is done for them speedily.*"

For the third day in a row, we hear about the distant coming of the Son of Man. The Gospel of Luke was written to bolster perseverance in a waiting people. This makes the promise of "speedy" salvation that much more remarkable. Salvation and its accompanying justice were to be Jesus' gift at his final coming. How could they come "speedily"?

One prominent theme in Luke is God's justice for the poor and downtrodden, even here and now, and God's summons to his people to reflect that faithfulness. Far from deferring salvation, this justice heralds its promised fullness.

When people feel powerless, when they've done all they can to effect change to no avail, it's tempting to rely on dramatic, divine intervention as their only recourse. On the other hand, when people tire of waiting, they try to set up the kingdom themselves. As John Lennon sang, they "imagine" heaven on earth without God. Neither approach reveals a realistic faith. Both lead to disappointment.

In this Gospel story, God sees to it that "justice is done." The use of the passive voice is telling. Without fanfare, God works through *us*, through the projects and institutions that he entrusts to us as reservoirs of *his* faithful love and saving power. The widow in today's Gospel might well have lived her whole life without being vindicated. When that happens today, it's not due to neglect by God, but to the sin even of believers whose piety is bereft of living, practical faith.

The widow is relentless. God's "chosen ones" *will* have their day in court. Jesus urges us to be with them, not with the defense. When he comes to establish the Father's kingdom, will he find prayerful faith that does justice? Or will he catch us sitting back, arms folded, waiting for him to do the work we should have done by his grace?

Oratio

Lord, the farther I go in the life of faith, the darker it gets. Unlike the stretch from point A to point B, the road of faith seems to lengthen, without an end in sight. May I hear your cries through my brothers and sisters in spiritual, physical, or material need. Then open my ears to hear your counsel and your promise to "receive me with honor" (Ps 73:24) after responding in faith to your daily comings.

Contemplatio

Clothe me with the robe of salvation; wrap me in the mantle of justice (see Is 61:10).

Thirty-Third Sunday of Ordinary Time— Year A

⋮ · · · · · · · · · · · · ⋮

Lectio

Matthew 25:14–30

Meditatio

"Should you not then have put my money in the bank . . . ?"

During my sophomore year at college my personal life was in disarray and my studies undisciplined. At one point I forgot that I had a test to study for. What a shock when I sat down in the classroom that morning! As I recall, the test consisted of about ten short essay questions. I think I answered three. The professor gave me an F and commented sadly, "If you had only written *something* instead of leaving all those blanks, I could have given you *some* credit."

I think that's what Jesus means when he tells the parable of the talents. If only the third servant had done something! Almost anything! Instead, he did nothing at all! That's why he was cast out.

What does this parable mean for us? It might mean doing more, but on the other hand our days may be very full, so it could be a question of doing one or two things *better*. Or this might be the time to launch a project we've dreamed about, for which we don't feel quite ready. Sometimes waiting to "be ready" means never to start at all. A priest I know likes to quote the line from G. K. Chesterton, "If a thing is worth doing, it is worth doing badly." When it's a religious and/or humanitarian project, something is usually better than nothing.

What matters is that we use the gifts God has given us— use them for God and for others. As Pope John Paul II said, although humans are the only beings that God created for their own sake, no one can really find himself or herself without making a sincere gift of self.

Where to begin? In our home, parish, or religious community, strengthening relationships? On the job, working more conscientiously? Or where? Where will the Spirit lead?

Oratio

Jesus, I want to make wise use of the gifts you have given me. I don't want to get stuck trying to make myself "ready." Please let me know when it's time to act. Inspire me how to better serve my family and/or my parish/religious community. (If I have a project in mind, help me to evaluate its worth, plan it out, find collaborators, and begin.) I want to make a sincere gift of myself to you and to my sisters and brothers.

Contemplatio

"Nothing ventured, nothing gained"—or, nothing ventured, something lost!

Thirty-Third Sunday of Ordinary Time—
Year B

❖ · · · · · · · · · · · ❖

Lectio

Mark 13:24–32

Meditatio

> *". . . when you see these things happening,*
> *know that he is near, at the gates."*

Today's Gospel is from Jesus' end-times discourse found near the end of Mark. Jesus speaks about the many signs and wonders that will indicate the end is near: a darkened sky, falling stars, and a moon without light. This is scary stuff! We don't usually see stars falling when we venture out into the night. Yet Jesus is not trying to scare us, but to challenge us to be attentive and watchful. He wants us to be prepared disciples, eager to welcome him at his coming, for time passes quickly and the day of salvation draws near.

This coming that Jesus speaks of cannot be understood only in terms of his final coming, his Parousia at the end of time. It can also be seen as any of his comings. For he comes every day in our ordinary lives, be it through a beautiful sunset or the encouraging words of a friend. And it is precisely in being attentive to, recognizing, and responding to these comings that I will be prepared for his ultimate and final coming.

So I need to ask myself: how attentive and watchful am I in my day-to-day life? How prepared am I for the Lord's "ordinary" and even subtle comings? Am I like the prudent virgin with lighted lamp and oil in hand, eagerly waiting for her Lord? Or am I, instead, like the fearful servant who buried his talent, afraid for his master's return? If I am the latter I need to ask myself, why do I fear the Lord's coming? Why do I hold back from his presence? Do I not love him? For if I do, then love casts out all fear. Love makes me attentive and watchful. Love makes me open and receptive to the many signs in my life that indicate his presence even now. And love gives me the strength to respond to this presence anew each day, for "he is near, at the gates."

Oratio

Jesus, the day passes quickly and the night is half-spent. You stand at my door knocking, eager to come in and sup with me. Help me to open my door wide, to welcome your presence fully and completely. For it is only then that I will breath fully and my heart will be satisfied.

Contemplatio

Come, Lord Jesus, do not delay!

Thirty-Third Sunday of Ordinary Time— Year C

∴· · · · · · · · · · · ·∴

Lectio

Luke 21:5–19

Meditatio

"It will lead to your giving testimony."

Near the end of the liturgical year, the Church provides Scripture readings to help us reflect on the end of the world and on our enduring hope that Jesus will come again at the end of time. Luke's description of these events is alarming. Jesus says that many awful things will happen, including persecution. But this persecution "will lead to your giving testimony." Jesus is clearly implying that giving testimony is a good thing, even though it comes in the midst of difficulties.

And the prediction of Jesus did come to pass. The Acts of the Apostles, the sequel to the Gospel of Luke, tells us about many occasions when the apostles give testimony. Often it is in the midst of persecution, such as when Peter and the other apostles are arrested (and then re-arrested after they escape from jail). Speaking for the rest, Peter gives testimony about the resurrection and exultation of Jesus, ending with, "We are witnesses of these things, as is the holy Spirit that God has given to those who obey him" (Acts 5:32).

Other testimony is given to curious bystanders, as in Peter's speech immediately after Pentecost. Stephen gives testimony before and as he is stoned to death. Paul gives testimony literally before governors and kings, as well as to bored intellectuals, superstitious pagans, and people of all walks of life who hunger for knowledge of God.

We, too, are called to give testimony, which means witnessing to our faith in Jesus. For us this won't usually involve speaking before governors and kings. But we can speak to our family and friends, to the curious or the hostile. Many things will lead to our giving testimony. Daily life provides the occasions, but it is for us to recognize them as opportunities.

Oratio

Jesus, giving testimony is usually difficult for me. I have a hard time talking about you to people. I'm afraid of what they will think. Give me the courage I need to witness to my faith in you—for I have been given the gift of faith in order to share it. And show me the people you want me to witness to. By myself I cannot do it, but with your Spirit in me, I trust that I can.

Contemplatio

I am your witness. Send me.

Monday of the Thirty-Third Week
of Ordinary Time

:·············:

Lectio

Luke 18:35–43

Meditatio

> *"The people walking in front rebuked him,
> telling him to be silent, but he kept calling out all the more. . . ."*

The Gospels often call our attention to the way that society treats the marginalized, in contrast to the way Jesus chooses to treat them. His genuine love, concern, and gentleness give us an example to embrace if we wish to call ourselves Christians. We know this, but we lose our way at times and seem to forget it, much like the crowd in today's Gospel.

At first, those in the crowd give the blind man the information that he seeks. They tell him that Jesus is the one causing all the uproar. But when the blind man tries to get Jesus' attention, they try to keep him quiet. In a sense they are turning on him; they want him to become "invisible" again.

The Gospel tells us that the blind man is sitting by the side of the road. Those in the crowd want to leave him there—they have their own agenda that day and it doesn't include this blind man stealing Jesus' attention from them. This reminds us of something else we might see on the side of the road today—rubbish. We leave what we no longer want, what we wish to forget, or what we have no use for on the side of the road, whether it's our garbage, an old couch, or a beggar.

Maybe each person in the crowd is hoping that Jesus will hone in on his or her need. Maybe the crowd simply wants to hear what Jesus is saying. Perhaps some of them have heard Jesus preach elsewhere or have heard others speak about him, but they are missing the point of discipleship. To be a disciple is to be concerned not just for one's own spiritual journey and formation, but to be aware of the others who are either on that journey or are being left on the side of the road.

Oratio

Sometimes, Lord, I get too absorbed in my needs and wants, and I fail to see the others on the road with me who are asking for my help and for yours. All these people are not just isolated individuals who happen to be traveling on the same path. You call us to something deeper. You invite us to notice one another, just as you notice us. Thank you for giving me to them, and them to me, so that we may be companions as we learn about love by loving one another. Amen.

Contemplatio

Lord, thank you for the companions you have given me on this journey.

Tuesday of the Thirty-Third Week
of Ordinary Time

∴∙∙∙∙∙∙∙∙∙∙∙∙∙∴

Lectio

Luke 19:1–10

Meditatio

> " . . . if I have extorted anything from anyone
> I shall repay it four times over."

He's short and can't see over the heads of the excited crowd pushing its way down the street, keeping pace with the teacher and healer in their midst. And—not being thin, since he's rich and eats well—he can't worm his way through that press of humanity. But he's determined to see Jesus. He runs ahead of the crowd, climbs into the low, welcoming branches of a sycamore and works his way up. As the crowd comes on, he waits—one arm wrapped around the strong trunk.

Then the unforgettable happens: "Zacchaeus, come down quickly, for today I must stay at your house!" The shocked crowd pulls apart to let Zacchaeus climb down, delighted but flustered. I think I know what's going through his mind: a meal provided by a person of dishonest wealth is considered contaminated. Everyone in the crowd knows this. Already the babble is subsiding and a strong murmur is swelling instead.

The portly little man stands stockstill and looks up into Jesus' smiling eyes. It's worth sacrificing just about anything to enjoy that smile for an hour or so. So Zacchaeus promises to right all of his unjust dealings. And Jesus immediately declares that salvation has come to the tax collector's house.

It seems to me that Zacchaeus wanted to see Jesus because he was looking for a new life. Money, a comfortable home, and sumptuous meals no longer satisfied him. His soul, like that of the psalmist, was thirsting for the living God. So he easily and sincerely promised to make restitution for his wrongs. That would be part of his new beginning.

I may need to make restitution, too—perhaps not money or goods, but another kind. I may be feeling remorse over an unkind remark I've made or a slight I've committed. Or there may be something else. In any case, I want to find a way to make up for the wrong. When I think of Jesus smiling at me in response, I know my "restitution" will be worthwhile.

Oratio

Jesus, Teacher and Healer, you call each of us by name and come to dwell among us. Each time I receive the Eucharist, you enter "my house." I wish it were swept and tidy! But, fortunately for me, you're willing to put up with the mess: my selfishness, my pride, my lack of charity, my addictions . . . . Under your calm and knowing gaze, may I start to put my life in order and make up for the wrongs I have done. I hope you will always be able to say of my soul: "Salvation has come to this house."

Contemplatio

What deed of restitution can I do today?

Wednesday of the Thirty-Third Week
of Ordinary Time

⟡ · · · · · · · · · · · · ⟡

Lectio

Luke 19:11–28

Meditatio

" . . . the Kingdom of God. . . ."

In today's Gospel, Luke tells us that Jesus is near Jerusalem. The people to whom he is speaking think of God's kingdom as a kingdom of earthly power, expecting it to immediately appear in Jerusalem. Their expectation is not fulfilled; they do not understand the true meaning of "kingdom of God."

It might be helpful to reflect on God's kingdom. Perhaps we do not think too often about it, or the differences between the kingdom of God and the kingdom proposed by many in our contemporary world. God's kingdom is characterized by love; humility; hope; care for the grieving, imprisoned, and poor; and living according to God's will and the other recommendations Jesus gave us. What values characterize the kingdom of this world?

We are surrounded by images, jingles, stories, and conversations that try to convince us that power, pleasure, and wealth are the ultimate goods, and that we should always look out for our own interests. We are so surrounded by these alluring voices touting the wonders of this world's kingdom that it can be difficult to see how they contrast with God's kingdom. Possessions, pleasure, and power are not bad in themselves. They cannot be an end in themselves, however, or we become restless and unfulfilled, and may even turn away from God. Rather, these things are to be used as a means to bring us to God.

Jesus tells the story of the noble who entrusted gold coins to some of his servants so that they could invest them for a profit. We have been entrusted with the treasure of Scripture, the Eucharist and the other sacraments, the Church, prayer, and the example of holy people. How do we value and use these gifts? Are we invested in using them for God's glory, our own good, and the good of others? May God enable us to use them wisely so that they bear much fruit in our lives and God's kingdom may reign!

Oratio

Loving and beloved God, may your kingdom come! May it flourish in this world, and may all people enjoy your kingdom in the world to come. I love you so much, and long to glorify you in all that I am and do. Enable me to recognize what is truly beautiful and valuable. Give me the wisdom and strength to choose you and whatever will lead me to you. I ask this in the name of Jesus. Amen.

Contemplatio

May your kingdom come, and may I seek it today.

Thursday of the Thirty-Third Week
of Ordinary Time

⁝ · · · · · · · · · · · · ⁝

Lectio

Luke 19:41–44

Meditatio

" . . . Jesus . . . wept . . ."

A church in the shape of a teardrop stands on the Mount of Olives in Jerusalem. It is called *Dominus Flevit*, "the Lord wept." A visitor to this church can look out and see the old city of Jerusalem nearby, and imagine Jesus weeping as he mourns for its people, who rejected him. This image of Jesus weeping over Jerusalem is one of the most poignant in the Gospels. The Greek word that Luke uses for "wept" *(klaiō)* doesn't just mean to cry in a gentle way. It expresses strong emotions, in the sense of bewailing. Jesus isn't just wiping a small tear from his eye. No, he's sobbing and lamenting over the fate of his beloved city, Jerusalem. He is looking toward the future, when the Romans will destroy the city and its Temple, which means everything to the Jews. The destruction of the Temple will be a terrible blow to them. To get a sense of it, imagine how we would feel if terrorists bombed Saint Peter's Basilica in Rome. To see that iconic image of the Catholic Church leveled to the ground would be devastating, even though we know the Church is not identified with any building.

Jesus, too, is not really weeping over the Temple building. He is weeping for the people, saying to them, "you did not recognize the time of your visitation." The visitation he speaks of is a special, divine intervention. Zechariah said at the Baptist's birth, "Blessed be the Lord, the God of Israel, for he has visited and brought redemption to his people" (Lk 1:68). God's visitation brings an outpouring of grace. To accept it is to accept the call to conversion and salvation. And what about me? Has God been trying to "visit" me lately? Is he calling me to a deeper conversion in my life? What is he asking of me now? Will I recognize and accept his invitation, happy to have him in my house? Or will I reject it—and give Jesus reason to weep anew, were that possible?

Oratio

Jesus, I hear your invitation: "Behold, I stand at the door and knock. If anyone hears my voice and opens the door, [then] I will enter his house and dine with him, and he with me" (Rev 3:20). Come into my house; I want to visit with you. You are always welcome. And I thank you for your invitation to come to your feast daily at the Eucharist. Lord, I am not worthy, but only say the word and I will be healed.

Contemplatio

Lord, help me recognize the time of your visitation.

Friday of the Thirty-Third Week of Ordinary Time

∴ · · · · · · · · · · · · ∴

Lectio

Luke 19:45–48

Meditatio

> *"Jesus entered the temple area and proceeded*
> *to drive out those who were selling things. . . ."*

Having sold religious books in the back of many a Catholic church in my time, I am especially eager to understand today's Gospel. In this chapter of Luke, Jesus is drawing near to Jerusalem with his disciples for the first time. He weeps over the city because its people don't recognize the time of their visitation. I imagine myself joining his group as we journey into the city itself.

Jesus walks into the Temple precincts, and turbulence ensues. He has returned to his Father's house (Lk 2:49) as the mature Teacher, ready to complete his Father's mission. Before taking up his rightful place to instruct the people, he must cleanse it. He drives out those who are selling things, using the holy place for their own gain. Even more, he desires to cleanse the hearts of all those who frequent there. The Gospel tells us further that the "chief priests, the scribes, and the leaders of the people, meanwhile, were seeking to put him to death . . . ." It doesn't seem that everyone in the crowd is well disposed to hear, understand, and take on the message. Those who are still plotting to kill him show us that we can be in a holy place or engaged in holy work, yet still miss out on the richness of all God wants to give us. Sadly, we can even reject it.

I stop to consider what Jesus' cleansing of the temple might mean for me today. How many things fill the temple of my heart and get in the way of the message? Small wonder the Gospel text actually says "selling things." Jesus' teachings have made me well aware of the lure of materialism. It is as much of a stumbling block now as it was in Jesus' day. What needs to be purged from my life so I can listen and live Jesus' message more fully? What will help me live as a disciple today?

Oratio

Jesus, help me see what needs to change in my life so that I may better listen to your word. You know me and understand me. You know how I can fill myself with things that won't really make me happy. I get stuck in them and I hold onto them. Help me recognize them today and let go, so I can better hold on to you.

Contemplatio

Lord, you desire to cleanse my heart. I desire that too.

Saturday of the Thirty-Third Week of Ordinary Time

:·············:

Lectio

Luke 20:27–40

Meditatio

"Some Sadducees . . . came forward and put this question to Jesus. . . ."

We hear two voices: the voice of the question meant to ensnare and destroy, and the voice of the Good Shepherd soon to become the Lamb of sacrifice. These two voices represent two other words that sound forth in the world in both hidden and obvious ways: the word of error that ends in illusion, and the Word of Truth, who knows us each by name. Daily we need to choose between these voices as guides for our lives.

Surfing the Internet: "No one will see what you're doing if you erase your history and password protect your e-mail. If no one gets hurt, it can't be wrong."

Parish life: "You're too busy to help out. Besides, you've done your part. Let the others take care of it."

An elderly parent: "It will be a change of lifestyle to take your mother into your home. You will have to give up a lot and reorganize your finances. But don't be fooled; it is really I who am knocking at your door."

Prayer: "I know you're busy. What about waking up five-minutes earlier to sit quietly and listen to my word?"

Through the Acts of the Apostles we see the down-to-earth struggle of the first Christians to listen attentively to the voice of the One whom they can no longer see. We can learn from them how to do it: daily they pray together and listen to the Word; they gather to discuss issues under the light of the Holy Spirit; they gather the communities together in love and care for one another, sharing all things in common; they listen to the apostles' preaching and reflect on their letters; they sing when imprisoned; and remain loyal to God in all things.

Oratio

May I hear your voice, O Lord. I have questions about what I should do right now in my life. Do you think that if I present them to you, you would help me out? I trust in you to lead me, to help me fulfill my duties in life, to strengthen me to fulfill my commitments. Attune my ears to your voice. Make it clear to me when I am being led by the duplicitous voice of the evil one. Lead me, Lord. Amen.

Contemplatio

Guide me. I long to hear your voice.

Christ the King—
Year A

:⋯⋯⋯:

Lectio

Matthew 25:31–46

Meditatio

"Whatever you did for one of the least . . . you did for me."

"Who, *him*?"

"I was supposed to help *her*?"

"Who, *me*?"

It can be pretty scary—thinking about the Last Judgment. How can we be sure we've done all we were supposed to do?

But if we sail on that tack, we might miss the entrance to the harbor. There's no way we can do all the good that can be done in the world. God's positive commands are open-ended, much more challenging than the "thou shalt nots." As thinking beings, we're asked to find our way, doing good to others without seriously neglecting our primary roles in life.

In the end, because we won't be sure how well we've done, we'll have to throw ourselves on the mercy of our all-knowing and understanding God. And that makes perfect sense. We're limited creatures. We don't have all the answers. To admit our ignorance is to be (at least, somewhat) humble, which is what God calls us to be—learning from his Son, who is meek and humble of heart (see Mt 11:29).

So we try to do our best, and let God do all the rest.

It's hard to "let God be God" and to let him guide us. As adults, we're so accustomed to making our own plans, even though we may ask advice from experts, friends, or family. To kneel or sit still and wait for the Lord's reply to our questions is foreign to our way of doing things. But sometimes the results can be amazing.

Shall we give it a try?

Oratio

Lord Jesus, I know that whatever I do to the least of your brothers and sisters I do to you. But I can't do all the good there is to be done in the world. So I ask you to help me sort it out—day by day, time by time. Please don't let me feel overwhelmed and paralyze myself so that I do nothing. I want to keep my priorities straight: I have to be faithful to the duties of my state in life and look after my well-being, without closing myself off from the needs of others. Please help me to find the balance that will be right for me and my dependents. And, above all, let whatever good I accomplish be done with you, and out of love of you and neighbor. Amen.

Contemplatio

You are my Lord and my God.

Christ the King—
Year B

:⋯⋯⋯:

Lectio

John 18:33b–37

Meditatio

> *"Everyone who belongs to the truth listens to my voice."*

Jesus gives a wonderful definition of a king: someone born to testify to truth. The Roman governor Pilate asks Jesus a direct question about his claim, "Then you are a king?" Jesus affirms it, "You say I am a king. For this I was born. . . ." Pilate must be shaking his head, however, because Jesus has already stated that his kingdom "does not belong to this world." Why, then, did he come into this world as king? The key lies in Jesus' next, curious statement, "I came into the world, to testify to the truth. Everyone who belongs to the truth listens to my voice."

Here is the dilemma. What does it mean to "belong to the truth?" Pilate is the example here. Jesus tries to bring him around indirectly. When Pilate asks him, "Are you the King of the Jews?" Jesus challenges Pilate's conscience by asking, "Do you say this on your own or have others told you about me?"

In other words, Jesus is telling Pilate that his opinion as governor is the only one that counts then and there. He holds the fate of Jesus in his hands. Pilate shoots back with his own challenge, "I am not a Jew, am I?" He reminds Jesus that the Jewish authorities who have handed him over should know the truth about him. Pilate should have taken the whole exchange more seriously because he will soon find himself shirking his duty to truth. Despite his doubts about Jesus' guilt, Pilate will choose the indecisive, self-serving, cowardly nonposition. He will wash his hands of guilt. And what would we do? The King of Truth is ours. Are we people of truth? Have we given ourselves completely to the truth by living out our baptism? Or are we disciples of Pilate, willing to acknowledge the existence of truth, but unwilling to belong to it totally? So many disciples pick and choose what teachings of the Gospel and of the Church they will accept. Will that style support us all the way through life? Will we end up owning the truth when we appear before the King, or will we try to defend our vacillation as did Pilate?

Oratio

Jesus, you are the Incarnate Truth. Continue to question me about my stance as disciple of truth. Do not let me falter or formulate my own definition of truth. I want to be able to stand tall before the world, a witness to my King. And I want to lay my heart humbly before you as servant of your truth. My trust is in your hands. Amen.

Contemplatio

Lord, you are the King of Truth and the King of my heart.

Christ the King—
Year C

❖ ⋯⋯⋯⋯⋯ ❖

Lectio

Luke 23:35–43

Meditatio

> "... *today you will be with me in Paradise.*"

Luke's account of the last moments of Jesus stresses the silence of our Savior in the face of so many threatening voices. He utters only three words to Pilate, "You say so" (Lk 23:3), and not a word to Herod. But Jesus promises paradise to the Good Thief. Jesus was wrongly and illegally sentenced to death, tortured, forced to carry his own cross to his execution, and even harassed by one of the criminals executed with him! He does not cry out for the right to a hearing, for he knows that hearing and listening are two very different things. He is simply silent before the powerful, just as the homeless and the poor are today. But Jesus did speak to the women on the way to Calvary who tried to comfort him with their weeping. Jesus entrusted women with the message of the crucifixion as well as that of the resurrection. Women remember, and they pass on to others what they remember. Jesus gave them the mandate to be prophets to future generations, announcing what they saw and heard, and passing on the message.

This is how the King of Kings acts. His every movement and word is etched on the collective memory of the Church. He leads his people through the gates of death, as a loving king guides his people through the dark valleys to higher ground. No generation has ever said: "This great, sad, loving drama has nothing to teach us." Every generation has said: "No one has ever spoken like this man" (see Jn 7:46). As I pray with this Gospel, I am there at Golgotha, there in Jesus' broken heart. Even in this extremity, Jesus thinks of others, because his entire existence can be summed up in the words: "For others." This is the way our Redeemer acts, our Redeemer who is our King.

Oratio

So much crowds my mind and heart as I wait with you in Gethsemane, Jesus. I want to shout my thanks, fidelity, love, and adoration. But like the apostles that fateful night, I remain mute. I mourn for the part that my own sin and sinfulness have played in this dark moment. Whatever I may have done, Jesus, I want to be with you as you suffer, and to grow in the faith that you have placed in my heart and soul, a faith I hope to share with all I meet.

Contemplatio

Our King has paid the price.

Monday of the Thirty-Fourth Week of Ordinary Time

Lectio

Luke 21:1–4

Meditatio

"She, from her poverty, has offered all. . . ."

When I was a teenager, I was at a Mass at which the great Cardinal Richard Cushing was seeking funds for the missions. We all laughed when he said "And I like silent collections!" In Jesus' time, there were no baskets, just big trumpetlike openings at the door of the Temple. Jesus sits opposite the collection stations and watches. He notices what certainly slips past the eyes of many others: an old woman surreptitiously drops her two copper coins into those giant openings, making a tiny tinkling sound. Jesus knows what does not meet the eye: those two coins were all she had to live on.

One can love and offer all even in the midst of corrupt systems and injustice. As Jesus watches our poor efforts at communal justice and fairness, which are so often tinged with original sin's sad legacy, he must remain as silent as he was at the Temple gate that day. All he can say is "Look out for the love that is found in the most unlikely places, from the most vulnerable people who do not seem to count for much."

Jesus tells me at the same time that I really do count, seldom for what I can do, which is so little, but always for who I am. Just as he watched that poor widow as if he were watching his own mother, he watches my every tiny effort to offer my love, my tears, my small contributions, my secret pains. When we let Jesus get close to us, big things sometimes start to happen. The day Cardinal Cushing preached at our parish church, I put my last quarter in the basket—no soda at the drugstore after Mass this time. . . . When I became a sister and was later sent to the missions for twenty years of service in Asia, the first thing I remembered was that quarter. Jesus didn't mind my noisy quarter, did he? I don't think Cardinal Cushing did, either!

Oratio

Jesus, I feel so close to those "widows" who can only put in a few coins and a little bit of energy into the great effort of spreading the Good News. Usually, if I am honest, I can only think of a tiny circle of others to whom I can be a witness for you. But your presence at the Temple gate that day gives me courage. Sometimes I see myself, my poverty and inability to take on the big issues, and forget about the important little issues that need to be faced if we are to build a Gospel world. Thank you for calling me to this, Jesus, and bless my littleness with much love.

Contemplatio

Watch for the love . . . .

Tuesday of the Thirty-Fourth Week
of Ordinary Time

⟡···········⟡

Lectio

Luke 21:5–11

Meditatio

> " . . . *the days will come when there will not be left*
> *a stone upon another stone. . . .*"

As we approach the conclusion of Ordinary Time, the readings become more ominous. They warn us of persecutions, the destruction of the Temple and of Jerusalem, and the end of the world. Rather than concentrating on the details of this passage, complex as it is even to scholars, let us dwell on two points. The first is that *all things come to an end*, and the second is to *focus our eyes on Jesus the Teacher*.

All things come to an end. When some people were marveling at the beauty of the Temple and its gifts, Jesus reminded them that it would all pass away with the Temple's destruction. Beauty is to be admired, but it is not wise to stake everything on it. Beauty is fleeting—whether a magnificent temple of worship, or the pleasant appearance of the temple of the human body, or any other form of beauty.

All glory and appreciation go to the divine Artist who created or inspired all beauty. If we concentrate on him, then when earthly beauty ends, we will still have divine loveliness to look forward to.

God's dwelling, the great Temple of Jerusalem that offered security and comfort to his people, was destroyed in the year A.D. 70 during the Romans' siege of the city. Our faith and confidence cannot be identified with material buildings, but with the God who fills them and all the universe.

When we have *our eyes fixed on Jesus* and do not follow false witnesses who pretend to take his place, we are assured of being protected even in the midst of external and internal turmoil. No matter the disorder and hardships that happen to us or around us, no matter the distressing end of beauty that we have enjoyed, if we remain true to Christ, we will walk securely.

Oratio

Jesus, you are the source of everything beautiful that I admire and enjoy. Thank you for the beauty all around me. When I see exquisite flowers, gorgeous sunsets, or lovely people, help me to see you in them. And when they fade, I will not fear, for you, Christ, are my Way, my Truth, and my Life. Even though everything may fall around me, my soul can rest secure in my faith and trust in you.

Contemplatio

"Persevere in running the race . . . while keeping our eyes fixed on Jesus" (Heb 12:2).

Wednesday of the Thirty-Fourth Week of Ordinary Time

❖ · · · · · · · · · · · · ❖

Lectio

Luke 21:12–19

Meditatio

> *"By your perseverance you will secure your lives."*

Who wants to reflect on persecution and possible martyrdom? Yet, here they are in today's Gospel. We can't honestly think that this passage isn't meant for us. So what can we take with us for today and the future?

I believe we can start with *humility*. Saint Augustine, painfully aware that many Christians had apostatized, wrote that we could never be sure that we'd have the strength to endure martyrdom. This thought, he said, should make us humble.

But then we can move on to *confidence*—not in ourselves, but in Jesus. In this same passage, the Lord says he will enlighten his followers as to what to say when brought before those hostile to the faith. This indicates that whatever might befall us, Jesus will be with us in our hour of need. But we have to ask for his help instead of caving in. We have to let him be enough for us. He is the Faithful One (see Rev 3:14).

Now we come to one of Luke's favorite words, *hypomonē*,

which translates into English as *perseverance* or *patient endurance.* At the end of this Gospel passage, Jesus tells us that by exercising this virtue we will secure our lives, being victorious even in death.

The twentieth century was an age of martyrs, and the twenty-first seems to be continuing the trend. But if we look at geography and percentages, most of us aren't likely to undergo martyrdom in the traditional sense. We can suffer other martyrdoms, however, such as patiently bearing intense pain, depression, loss of independence, or deprivation of cherished possessions—situations that may accompany advancing age or result from unfortunate circumstances.

In such situations, by humbly trusting in Jesus, the Faithful One, and persevering in the good, Christ's followers will secure their lives.

Oratio

Jesus, Lord, you are the Faithful One, living and true. I trust you to be with me in my hours of greatest need. May I never think that I'm alone, even if I can't sense your presence, even if I'm experiencing a spiritual night. May I turn to you for strength in the dark and difficult days that I'm going through now or that may come in the future. With your presence and support, I can get through anything!

Contemplatio

Lord, lead me on.

Thursday of the Thirty-Fourth Week of Ordinary Time

⁝··········⁚

Lectio

Luke 21:20–28

Meditatio

> *". . . stand erect and raise your heads. . . ."*

"Stand up straight!" Judging from how often parents say the same things, you'd think that every newborn comes into the world with an instruction manual: Don't slouch; you'll get rounded shoulders. Don't cringe; you're asking for trouble. Look the world in the eye; you'll project that you know who you are and that you're worth respecting.

In recounting Jesus' teaching on his final coming, Luke connects two events, the end of the world and the end of *a* world, the fall of Jerusalem. Jesus uses the destruction of Jerusalem as his platform for a wider discussion about the fulfillment of the world. Those who reject him are themselves paving the way for the destruction of all they treasure. Their loss is not as much from God's condemnation as from the logical consequence of their choice to eliminate the Lord of Life from their lives. On a brighter note, far from being dismayed, perplexed, and frightened, those who believe and follow Christ can "stand erect and raise [their] heads," because all they hoped and lived for is about to come true.

Even if we feel we're on the winning side, such apocalyptic fare can be hard to digest. It helps to distinguish between Christ's teaching and its style. Despite the alarming imagery inside or outside the Gospel, his prediction is peace.

One effect of standing up straight is the confidence we have to share that peace with others. This is the purpose of Christian mission, Christian liturgy, and every Christian's life. Living in virtue and going to heaven are not enough. We have been charged with patiently, courageously, and skillfully preparing the whole world, especially our corner of it, for the final coming of Christ.

Oratio

Lord, I entrust myself to you as *ho eschatos*, the Final One. No one else and nothing else lays such claim to my heart. As wonderful as this world is, its ultimate meaning is in you. Sometimes silently, sometimes with a roar, my world "disappears." It frightens me, because I don't know anything else. Help me remember that nothing else matters when I compare it with you. At the same time though, because it's in you, it does matter. The future kingdom is like a seedling in the world, and just as you're present in our lives now, so you'll be there for us all at the end.

Contemplatio

I remember, and so I hope.

Friday of the Thirty-Fourth Week
of Ordinary Time

∴· · · · · · · · · · · ·∴

Lectio

Luke 21:29–33

Meditatio

> " . . . *know that the Kingdom of God is near.* . . ."

This passage has always been a bit difficult for me to grasp, perhaps because of its cryptic language. It follows several descriptions of the end of the world and the destruction of Jerusalem. The scenes painted in the preceding passage are horrific. It ends with signs to help readers know when they can expect the prophecy to be fulfilled, along with a word of encouragement. Those who would have heard this language had probably also heard the stories passed down for several generations about the destruction of Jerusalem, which had occurred 600 years previously. If I had been one of the persons hearing this, I would have been terrified.

Yet, the metaphor Jesus uses in today's Gospel is beautiful and hopeful. He could have used a different metaphor: "Consider the cedar of Lebanon and all the other trees. When their limbs begin to bow under the wind, know that a hurricane is now near." Under the circumstances, would not this metaphor be a bit more apropos? But no, not in God's mind. The metaphor God offers for our consideration is about a fig tree bursting open with new life in the springtime, which shows that summer is near.

Jesus is saying that we live in a world of extreme uncertainty. We see many signs around us reminding us of the death and destruction that could touch us at any moment. This reality, however, is not the only reality in which we are submerged. We are also submerged in the reality called the kingdom of God.

No matter what we experience now or may experience in the future, the kingdom of God is close. Its reality must capture our imaginations so we do not let terror overwhelm us, but live in the hope of knowing that the kingdom of God is near.

Oratio

Jesus, I can relate to the people who heard you speak these words. When I read about things like earthquakes, hurricanes, tsunamis, mass shootings, it's hard to focus on the positive. Thank you for reminding me that a more powerful reality operates even in the midst of death and destruction. Even more, thank you for allowing me to be a part of your kingdom so I have something to lean on should I, or anyone I love, ever experience one of these disasters. Help me to see signs of your kingdom everywhere. Amen.

Contemplatio

Lord, show me the signs of your kingdom in my life.

Saturday of the Thirty-Fourth Week of Ordinary Time

❖ · · · · · · · · · · · · ❖

Lectio

Luke 21:34–36

Meditatio

> *"Beware that your hearts do not become drowsy. . . ."*

The end is near! Today is the last day of Ordinary Time. Tomorrow the season of Advent begins, the opening of a new liturgical year. Jesus' words are appropriate for this end of the year. He speaks about having a drowsy heart, which he explains as allowing self-indulgence and the cares of our daily lives to use up the energy of our hearts. The image of a tired heart, barely beating, comes to mind. Jesus warns us about having a drowsy heart because when we are tired, we become disoriented and do not see clearly.

The end of this liturgical year is a good time to take stock of our hearts. We can ask ourselves, "What preoccupies my heart?" Is it something as mundane as what I will have for dinner? Or have I lost my job and wonder how I'll pay my bills? Do I lose my peace when someone cuts in front of me in the checkout line or beats me to a great parking spot? On the other hand, am I preoccupied with how my family will fit Sunday Mass and soccer into this weekend? If I was not able to give aid to that homeless person asking for help, did I offer a prayer for him or her as I passed by? Jesus isn't telling us that concerns and cares are useless; rather, he wants us to entrust ourselves to him. Otherwise, if we become the central focus of everything and fail to put our trust in the Father, we can lose sight of others and ignore our brothers and sisters in need. We can forget that a more glorious place awaits us, a place where we can "stand before the Son of Man." However, before we get there, he wants us to be vigilant in order to be his presence in our world.

Oratio

Lord, as I end this liturgical year, I reflect on your gracious love. You have held me up when I was too weak to stand. You provided guidance in your word. You showed me the way to live and act by the example of your selfless life. Help me to not give up when I see my weakness, but continue to face the cares and temptations that drain my heart, relying on you. As I enter into the season of Advent, may I live in the hope of your love and mercy.

Contemplatio

"Be vigilant . . . and pray that you have the strength . . . to stand before the Son of Man."

Solemnities and Feasts
of the Lord and the Saints

Transfiguration of the Lord—August 6
Year A

:·············:

Lectio

Matthew 17:1–9

Meditatio

" . . . *Jesus came and touched them.* . . ."

The evangelists tell us that Jesus liked to pray at night. He would commune with his Father in the relative isolation of darkness. It was probably night on that mountaintop when the Master went a short distance apart from his three companions and began to pray. Did the apostles sleep meanwhile? Matthew doesn't tell us so, but according to Luke they did. Imagine waking up and seeing Jesus' face shining "like the sun," his garments glowing, and two strange figures standing with him! It's no wonder the apostles were frightened.

The vision vanished, and in the darkness the apostles heard footsteps approaching. Then Jesus touched them reassuringly. "Rise," he said, "and do not be afraid." They were not to fear because Jesus was with them, as his touch assured them. It's a detail only Matthew mentions, and it's consistent with one of the themes of his Gospel. In chapter 1, Matthew identifies Jesus as Emmanuel, God-with-us. In chapter 28, Matthew quotes Jesus' promise to be with his followers until the end of time. This theme recurs throughout the Old and New Testaments in various wordings: "I am with you." "I will be with you to deliver you." "It is I." Usually it's linked with: "Do not be afraid," as in this transfiguration account.

The apostles aren't the only persons whom Jesus assures of his presence; he assures us, too. He's with us in our sleeping, in our waking, and in our daily round of activity. He wants to encourage us: "Don't worry; don't be anxious. I'm here. I'm with you."

Let's cultivate a deeper awareness of this reality now, so that when difficult moments come, we won't falter. We want to remain firm in the conviction that the Lord is ready to come to our rescue.

Oratio

Lord Jesus, you are Emmanuel, God-with-us. You will be with us always, until the end of time and beyond. And you will be not only with your people, the Church—but also with each of us individually. You are with me now and will be with me in the future. Help me to deepen this conviction, so that in times of loss, grief, confusion, anxiety, or dread I may turn to you with trust. At such moments, may I at least manage to pray, "Lord, please get me through this." I know that you'll take over from there.

Contemplatio

"Do not be afraid."

Transfiguration of the Lord—August 6
Year B

⋮· · · · · · · · · · · · ·⋮

Lectio

Mark 9:2–10

Meditatio

"Jesus . . . led them up a high mountain apart by themselves."

The Gospels mention instances when Jesus either goes off somewhere by himself or calls the apostles apart with him. The reason for this time apart is twofold: to have the time and space to meet with God, and to be renewed by that divine encounter. In this passage Jesus invites Peter, James, and John to come away with him so as to facilitate an encounter that becomes a theophany (seeing a glorified Jesus). But why does Jesus want them to have this experience?

Relationships between two people—be they husband and wife, or friends—cannot truly thrive unless the persons spend quality time together. During these sacred times we come to greater intimacy and each person gets to know the other one better.

Jesus is inviting the three apostles, and us, to come apart from the group so that during this "quality time" he can make himself better known. Because they are alone with Jesus they can hear a clear instruction from the Father, "Listen to him." Deeper knowledge of Jesus and the Father is a direct result of coming apart and stepping away from other distractions. The message the Father gives is the fruit of this quality time the apostles spend with their Lord.

We, like the apostles, have a need for "time alone" with our God. In fact he invites us precisely to this so that our relationship with him can grow and deepen. Certainly we encounter him in times of prayer like the one right now (a prayer in which we talk as well as listen—as if sitting down to a cup of coffee with someone we love). But other times can also be fruitful quality times, such as a retreat. We can then spend an extended amount of time listening to God with open hearts as he reveals himself and his message to us.

Oratio

Jesus, just as you called the three apostles apart, today you call me to greater intimacy with you. I want to respond. As I sit here quietly for the next five or ten minutes, show me where I can steal ten minutes, a half hour, or an hour to spend with you each day. Give me the grace of an open and loving heart directed to you, one which readily responds to you. Thank you, Lord, for the great gift you offer me in calling me to a more profound relationship with you, my God— my answer is *yes!*

Contemplatio

Lord, it is good to be here with you.

Transfiguration of the Lord—August 6
Year C

⁘ · · · · · · · · · · · · ⁙

Lectio

Luke 9:28b–36

Meditatio

"Master, it is good that we are here. . . ."

Luke places this radiant event in the context of prayer.
Jesus invites his closest friends to come with him up Mount
Tabor. For Jesus, the mountains are significant places of
encounter with God, places of prayer and preaching: Olivet,
Tabor, Calvary. Clearly, we are in the presence of mystery as
Jesus' face and garments are made luminous and glory shines
around him. Moses and Elijah, who similarly had mountaintop experiences of God, are seen conversing with Jesus. As
the prophets are leaving, Peter and the others catch a glimpse
of them. Awestruck and incredulous, they want to set up
tents, as if in some way they might capture the moment and
enter more deeply into it.

Immediately a cloud (signifying the presence of God)
casts a shadow over them and draws them within. The messianic significance of the cloud should not be overlooked.
(See Ex 16:10; 19:9; 33:9; 1 Kgs 8:10–11). The privileged
words the three disciples hear are significant for them and for
us: "This is my chosen Son; listen to him." Of all the recom-

mendations or directives that could have been given, the disciples are told to *listen!*

The disciples did not earn or deserve this experience. It is a gift meant to strengthen and support their faith. Trials await them as they follow Jesus into Jerusalem, where he will face his passion. Later, they will be called to witness to what they have seen and heard, but now they need only *listen.*

Perhaps we can recall certain graced moments of prayer when the Lord consoled or reassured us with his presence and peace. It is good to silence our hearts and enter fully into these experiences since, like the disciples, we too will have to come down from the mountain and face times of trial and temptation. It is encouraging to remember, however, that the Lord is near not only on the mountaintops, but in the highways and byways of our earthly journey of life.

Oratio

Thank you, Lord, for the many ways you continue to reveal yourself to us. Your invitation to prayer and the gift of your divine presence dwelling in both word and sacrament, as well as in our hearts, continually renew and strengthen your Church on its pilgrim journey. Help me to listen more deeply to your inspirations. Let these illuminate and guide all my decisions and actions as I seek to conform my life to yours. May I enjoy the full vision of your glory one day in heaven with the angels and saints and all my loved ones!

Contemplatio

"Listen to him."

Assumption of the Blessed Virgin Mary
August 15

:⋯⋯⋯⋯:

Lectio

Luke 1:39–56

Meditatio

"And Mary said. . . ."

With the quick steps of youth, Mary approaches the home of Elizabeth and Zechariah. I picture a plain, mud-brick wall with a doorway in the middle. The door is open because it's daytime. As Mary approaches, clucking chickens scatter. She enters, stepping into a dirt-floored courtyard that has rooms on three sides. When she calls out the traditional greeting, Zechariah, who has been dozing against the shaded wall, straightens up, startled. And Elizabeth emerges from the storeroom, her face alight with joy.

What Luke relates next is very interesting. He tells us that as Elizabeth began to utter those well-known prophetic words, "Blessed are you," she was filled with the Holy Spirit. Farther on, Luke will tell us that both Simeon and Anna were filled with the Spirit on the day of Jesus' presentation. However, when Mary breaks into her *Magnificat*, Luke simply states: "And Mary said . . . ."

This was pointed out to me years ago, and I still marvel at it. The Spirit, who, like the wind, usually "blows where it wills" (see Jn 3:8), was inspiring Mary all the time, so Luke does not state: "And, filled with the Holy Spirit, Mary said. . . ."

Hers was a special grace, of course. We could never hope to attain a union with the Holy Spirit as close as Mary's. Yet each of us can grow in holiness. Through Mary's intercession, let us ask the Spirit for an increase of faith, hope, love, and the gifts that will make us receptive to his inspirations. We can ask for the graces we need in order to correct what we know needs correction. And, because we never know ourselves fully, we can also ask for those unknown graces by which God wants to realize the dream he has for us.

Oratio

Mary, Mother of Jesus and my mother, obtain for me a strong devotion to the Holy Spirit. Intercede for me with the Spirit, that I may develop a firmer faith, a brighter hope, a more ardent love for God and others. Ask the Spirit to make me more sensitive—more receptive—to the light and strength he wants to give me day by day. I know I need these graces *(name them)*, and I also ask for the graces the Spirit is ready to give that I'm unaware of needing. I want to be a better witness to Jesus, your Son and my Brother. Amen.

Contemplatio

Hail, Mary . . . .

Triumph of the Cross
September 14

∴∙∙∙∙∙∙∙∙∙∙∙∙∴

Lectio

John 3:13–17

Meditatio

"For God so loved the world. . . ."

Back in the mists of history, in the beauty of the primeval garden, God loved the world he had created. He loved the fragile creatures he had made on the sixth day: the man and the woman he placed in the garden. Day after day he strolled with them through this beautiful garden. How pleasant the conversations they enjoyed together.

After the man and woman became suspicious that God was hiding something from them, after they tried to find their own way to power and control, love took on a new name: *mercy*. God promised them redemption. He carefully sewed leather clothes for them, for they had used only fig leaves to cover their nakedness. He walked through the rest of history with his human creatures, seeking them out, protecting them, guiding them, saving them, taking pity on them. I wonder how sharply he missed those first days of intimacy and trust in the garden.

To Moses he declared his name: I am with you, near you always. To David, God promised his house would forever sit on his throne. Through the prophets, he painted for his people a picture of future salvation: the Suffering Servant, new life in dead bones, a promise to rescue the lame and restore the fortunes to his people in exile, and to fill his people with his spirit. And now Jesus proclaims again the mercy of his Father. "Just as Moses lifted up the serpent in the desert [to heal the people], so must the Son of Man be lifted up, so that everyone who believes in him may have [not just temporal but] eternal life."

Oratio

Father, my Father, what a privilege to be able to call you my Father, a gift, a grace, an inestimable blessing. Father . . . it is a word of relationship. Jesus proclaimed your love, but it has been clear to us from the very beginning. As we seek to run from you, you run after us by sending us your Son, not to condemn us but to save us. You wait for us patiently, you desire us, you seek us, you show us your face in his kindness and compassionate forgiveness. You are like a parent wild with anxiety when a child is lost, who offers extravagant sums as a reward for finding the lost one. You have offered more than an extravagant sum—you have handed over your beloved Son for your erring children, that all might be once more safe in the garden of your love and care. Father, my Father, our Father, deliver us from evil. Amen.

Contemplatio

My Father, my Father, you have loved us always.

All Saints
November 1

:⋯⋯⋯:

Lectio

Matthew 5:1–12a

Meditatio

"Blessed are you. . . ."

When Jesus sees the crowds, he goes up the mountain and begins to teach. He has something special to say, which needs to be proclaimed solemnly, as Moses had proclaimed the Ten Commandments. When I read Jesus' Beatitudes, his thinking amazes me. His ideas were unheard-of in Palestine where he preached, and they are still unheard-of today. Just stop to think about the messages we get from TV commercials, store windows, or news reports on the wars we wage.

Jesus speaks about eight human situations, things that we might be living through right now, like grief, poverty, mercy. Then Jesus promises even more—that we will belong to the kingdom of heaven, that all the effort we make to walk the straight and narrow will be worth it. It is as if Jesus is telling us "I see it all. I know what you bear, the burden you struggle under. Have courage, because these difficulties are your tickets to blessedness in the kingdom."

I don't think that Jesus is telling us that God asks a price for everything, but that our daily troubles will mold us into blessedness. The effort to keep my heart clean will make my vision sharper to see and enjoy the sights of God's kingdom. My mourning over deceased loved ones will be totally replaced by the joy of meeting them in the kingdom. I think of the homeless, who will certainly inherit the land; those unjustly imprisoned, who will be free to walk the halls of the Father's dwelling; those who have forgiven, who will be placed close to Jesus, their model of forgiveness and mercy. I am strengthened every time I read the Beatitudes, for they seem to tell me: rejoice, because the heavenly reward will be great. What a promise!

Oratio

Jesus, I believe in your promises, given so solemnly on the mountain. I ask you to stay by my side, because I am far from those beautiful dispositions of humility, mercy, righteousness, and good heart that form the core of your Beatitudes. Help me to think of them on the street, in the supermarket, at a coffee klatch, in the office, on the train, at the dinner table—every place that I share your world with my brothers and sisters . . . and you. Amen.

Contemplatio

Rejoice and be glad!

All Souls
November 2

:··········•:

Lectio

John 11:17–27

Meditatio

". . . he who believes in me, even if he dies, will live. . . ."

It is difficult—this meeting between Jesus and Martha of Bethany. She had hoped (perhaps expected) that he would arrive before Lazarus died. Now she sees no possibility that her brother will return to life, because so much time has elapsed since his death.

Jesus knows why he has delayed his arrival, but his own emotions are churning within him as he tries to calmly assure Martha that all will be well. After a brief dialogue, Martha professes her belief in Jesus as Messiah. Soon afterward, Jesus works the miracle that will lead to his own death.

"He who believes in me," Jesus tells Martha, "even if he dies, will live." This truth should console us as we celebrate the feast of All Souls. Our loved ones who believed are, or will be, enjoying eternal life! They'll be waiting for us to join them in never-ending bliss.

Grieving is only natural. But for us Christians it's more often for ourselves, who will miss the deceased, than for our departed loved ones. As Saint Paul says, our dear ones have run the race and finished the course (see 2 Tm 4:6–8). Those of us they've left behind are still "running," and without them beside us. So we experience a profound sense of loss.

Throughout our lives, we have to confront many kinds of losses. We experience physical and emotional separations, as well as loss of youth, lessening of strength, loss of skills, lapses of memory, failing senses, detachments from possessions. . . . The list goes on and on. During young adulthood and middle age, losses might actually allow new opportunities to open up. The losses that take place in one's senior years can be painful, but they may help one to grow in faith and hope and become more firmly grounded in God's love. A person might even decide that nothing else really matters.

Oratio

Father, Son, and Holy Spirit, I entrust to you my departed loved ones. Lead them into eternal life, so they may enjoy your presence forever. Help me, as I remain behind, to mourn their loss and then move on, believing and hoping that I will again enjoy their company. As my losses multiply with the passing of the years, please help me to endure them patiently and perhaps find substitutes for some of these deprivations. In any case, enable me to understand that what really matters is your unconditional love. Guide me in your paths and keep me faithful. Amen.

Contemplatio

God's love matters most.

Dedication of the Basilica of Saint John Lateran
November 9

⁝· · · · · · · · · · · ·⁝

Lectio

John 2:13–22

Meditatio

> " . . . *the temple of his body.*"

Why on earth do we celebrate a building? Granted, as the pope's cathedral on Lateran Hill, it's "the first church in Christendom." Not even iconic Saint Peter's Basilica claims as much. But it's still just stone and bronze. The church is officially named "Archbasilica of the Most Holy Savior and Saints John the Baptist and John the Evangelist." (The name "Lateran" comes from the Roman family who originally owned the land.)

Not long ago, a language student in Rome managed to make it to Saint John Lateran for the evening high Mass on this very day. Afterward, she exited the central door, which had been opened for the occasion. Since the crowd was gone, she turned back for a last glance. The lights in the apse had remained on—another rarity. The high altar throbbed with the glow, and the blaze coursed down the nave and spilled out onto the darkened piazza, into the world and its ways.

Suddenly that basilica, like every church, symbolized for her the pulsing life of Christ's risen body that John alludes to in today's Gospel. Jesus stands prophetically in his Father's purified Temple and dares his challengers, aghast at his affront, to keep him down. Their ripening hatred would only provide the way for God to unleash the Spirit onto the world, and humanity would once again become a living being (see Gn 2:7)—only this time it would be Christ's body, extended far beyond their wildest dreams.

It is this body, represented by the liturgical assembly, that gives life to a church. The Church, the body of Christ, can exist without buildings, but it can never exist without this assembly. Conceived on the cross and in the empty tomb, it is born in Baptism and takes shape in the Eucharist. ". . . [W]e were all baptized into one body" (1 Cor 12:13); ". . . we, though many, are one body, for we all partake of the one loaf" (1 Cor 10:17). Now *that's* something to celebrate.

Oratio

Jesus, Paul reminds us that your Spirit dwells in us as in a temple (see 1 Cor 3:16). Like Saint Augustine, who urged us to be what we are, Paul speaks to us not as islands, but as Christians together, your body. Your risen body is glorified. Let that Spirit-filled body be the way for our faith, our conversations, our decisions, and our mutual love and care, as together we make our way to glory. May those who see our "body" see yours, be blessed with your presence, and come to share fully in this unity.

Contemplatio

"You are the temple of God" (1 Cor 3:16).

List of Contributors

∴ . . . . ∴

Celebrate the Church's great seasons of grace by praying
lectio divina with the Daughters of St. Paul.

ADVENT GRACE
Daily Gospel Reflections
By the Daughters of St. Paul
0-8198-0787-7
$7.95

LENTEN GRACE
Daily Gospel Reflections
By the Daughters of St. Paul
0-8198-4525-6
$7.95

Continue to celebrate the grace of God in everyday life
through *lectio divina* with the Daughters of St. Paul.

ORDINARY GRACE
Weeks 1–17
Daily Gospel Reflections
By the Daughters of St. Paul
0-8198-5442-5
$9.95

ORDINARY GRACE
Weeks 18–34
Daily Gospel Reflections
By the Daughters of St. Paul
0-8198-5443-3
$9.95

Order at www.pauline.org, or by calling Pauline Books & Media at
1-800-876-4463, or through the book and media center nearest you.

BOOKS & MEDIA

A mission of the Daughters of St. Paul

As apostles of Jesus Christ, evangelizing today's world:

We are CALLED to holiness
by God's living Word and Eucharist.

We COMMUNICATE the Gospel message
through our lives and through all
available forms of media.

We SERVE the Church
by responding to the hopes and needs
of all people with the Word of God,
in the spirit of St. Paul.

For more information visit our website:
www.pauline.org.

BOOKS & MEDIA

The Daughters of St. Paul operate book and media centers at the following addresses. Visit, call or write the one nearest you today, or find us on the World Wide Web, www.pauline.org

CALIFORNIA

3908 Sepulveda Blvd, Culver City, CA 90230	310-397-8676
935 Brewster Avenue, Redwood City, CA 94063	650-369-4230
5945 Balboa Avenue, San Diego, CA 92111	858-565-9181

FLORIDA

145 S.W. 107th Avenue, Miami, FL 33174	305-559-6715

HAWAII

1143 Bishop Street, Honolulu,HI 96813	808-521-2731
Neighbor Islands call:	866-521-2731

ILLINOIS

172 North Michigan Avenue, Chicago, IL 60601	312-346-4228

LOUISIANA

4403 Veterans Memorial Blvd, Metairie, LA 70006	504-887-7631

MASSACHUSETTS

885 Providence Hwy, Dedham, MA 02026	781-326-5385

MISSOURI

9804 Watson Road, St. Louis, MO 63126	314-965-3512

NEW YORK

150 East 52nd Street, New York, NY 10022	212-754-1110

PENNSYLVANIA

Philadelphia—relocating	215-676-9494

SOUTH CAROLINA

243 King Street, Charleston,SC 29401	843-577-0175

VIRGINIA

1025 King Street, Alexandria, VA 22314	703-549-3806

CANADA

3022 Dufferin Street, Toronto, ON M6B 3T5	416-781-9131

¡También somos su fuente para libros, videos
y música en español!